Middle School

Published by Familius LLC, www.familius.com
PO Box 1249, Reedley, CA 93654

Familius books are available at special discounts for bulk purchases,
whether for sales promotions or for family or corporate use.
For more information, contact Familius Sales at orders@familius.com.

Library of Congress Control Number: 2022936579

Print ISBN 9781641706636
Ebook ISBN 9781641706872

Printed in the United States of America

Edited by Lindsay Sandberg, Sarah Echard, and Spencer Skeen
Cover design by Mara Harris
Book design by Mara Harris

10 9 8 7 6 5 4 3 2 1
First Edition

Middle School

Safety Goggles Advised

Jessica Speer

FAMILIUS

For all middle schoolers—past, present, and future.
May the Force be with you.

Contents

Introduction:

A Formula for . . . Well, Weird Stuff in Middle School

• •

Warning:

Read with caution if you are prone to nausea, hives, or vomiting. This book dissects the weird stuff that happens in middle school, which can be messy. Some of this weirdness you've likely experienced firsthand. Some you've heard about or witnessed. And a rare few of you live in a world of rainbows and unicorns. Safety goggles and a sense of humor recommended. By the end of the book, rest assured, you'll have a better understanding of yourself, your fellow humans, and how to play a role in creating positive change.

The (Not Very) Scientific Formula for Middle School:

Step 1: Take a large group of kids in puberty.

Step 2: Combine them in a new school.

Step 3: Blend with a complicated schedule of classes and new teachers. Add a generous dose of tests, homework, and hormones.

Step 4: Pour into a packed lunchroom filled with diverse personalities, bland food, and unpleasant odors. Heat to 400 degrees.

It's no wonder that what emerges is some pretty strange stuff! Not to mention stress. Yes, there are cool things about middle school, like more independence, new friends, and new activities. But there's baffling stuff too, like harsh judgment, the whole "popularity" thing, and, of course, drama. These behaviors range from awkward to annoying to painful.

With insights from hundreds of students, this book explores the halls of middle school, especially the odd behaviors that lurk in the shadows. Slip on your lab coats, because we're going to dissect these behaviors one by one to understand what's *really* going on.

We'll shed light on *why* there's so much judgment, *why* some kids are obsessed with popularity, *what's up* with dating, and much more. But most importantly, this book will help you deal and define *how you want to be*. Middle school only lasts a few years, but it's a good place to explore who you are and how to navigate life when things get, well, weird.

Laboratory Instructions: Read Before You Begin

You are about to enter a scientific exploration of middle school. Unlike reading a typical book, this experience may drum up awkward memories, unexpected emotions, or the sudden urge to hide in the closet. Do not fear. Push through these uncomfortable reactions, as the end result is worth it. By digging into strange middle school behaviors, you will emerge more equipped to deal with them. (Or, possibly, you will be hiding in the closet.)

Grab a pencil, because each chapter includes hands-on activities to gather your experiences and insights. Your active participation will help to shed light on this complex social experiment known as middle school. (Lucky you! You are now a participant in this scientific journey.)

Chapter Guide: What to Expect

Each chapter follows a (not very) scientific method to carefully dissect ten common middle school experiences. Key sections include:

Research Questions

Chapters begin with a few simple questions for you to answer. These questions are designed to get you thinking about your personal experiences with each topic. Simply be honest. There are no right or wrong answers.

Under the Microscope:
What's Really Going On

From there, the hidden reasons driving strange behaviors are explained through the insights of middle schoolers and a dash of science.

You Choose the Ending

Then, a typical middle school scenario gives you the chance to decide how you might respond in that situation. As in real life, navigating these scenarios is tricky. There are no "correct" responses, since life is unpredictable and everyone's different. If you don't like any of the endings, create your own.

Antidotes from Middle Schoolers:
How to Deal

Students then share advice on how to deal with tricky situations and behaviors. Feel free to add your insights to this collection of sage advice.

Important Stuff & The Final Word

At the end of each chapter, the main findings are summarized in these two sections.

Challenge for Change

If you would like to dig deeper into topics, each chapter includes two challenges to explore your own actions and activities to prompt change.

Scientific and Random Facts

Scattered throughout the book are relevant and totally irrelevant facts for your reading pleasure.

Okay, slap on your latex gloves and grab your scalpel. Let the middle school dissection begin!

Chapter 1:

Weird Behavior #1— Harsh Judgment

• •

Okay, please clear your desk and take out a pencil. Do your best, and *do not* look at your neighbor's answers.

Ugh! Not another test, you're thinking.

Don't panic. This isn't for a grade. And there are no right answers. Truly! Think of this as scientific research. All you have to do is *honestly* answer three simple questions.

(This Is NOT a Test) Research Questions:

	YES	NO
Have you ever made an assumption about someone you didn't know well, like "She's bossy," "He thinks he's better than everyone," or "That person is weird"?	☐	☐

	YES	NO

Have you ever thought something about somebody but then realized you were *totally wrong?* ☐ ☐

Have you ever shared your opinion about another kid, but if that kid ever heard what you said, you would *feel terrible?* ☐ ☐

If you answered YES to any of these, *that's judgment.* Despite our best efforts, we ALL judge others. Our brains are hardwired to make automatic judgments.

Disclaimer:

Okay, there may be a few superhumans on this planet that do not have judgmental thoughts—such as your Great Aunt Betty—but pretty much the rest of us do. We're human, after all.

Judgment Under the Microscope: What's Really Going On

Here's a (not very) scientific illustration of how quickly the human brain makes judgments:

Imagine you are walking home from school one sunny day. You notice a cute dog sitting by a fence. It looks friendly. As you move to pet the dog, it snarls and snaps at you. You jump back and no longer think the dog is cute. It's mean!

But then you notice it has one of its hind legs caught in a wire. Now you feel bad because you can see it's in pain.

Is anyone feeling a bit of whiplash? In a matter of seconds, you went from thinking the dog was nice to mean to suffering. Hmmm . . . either that dog experiences extreme mood swings or your brain made some snap judgments.

Clarification: It's important to note that judgment is not necessarily negative. For example:

Good judgment = deciding not to take a selfie with the grizzly bear you stumble upon while hiking.

Harsh judgment = making fun of anyone who has freckles or likes the color yellow. (This chapter focuses on this type of judgment.)

Believe it or not, these snap judgments trace back to the survival instincts of early humans. Imagine the daily threats they faced, like saber-toothed tigers, ice ages, and no cell phones. To survive, the human brain evolved to judge things, especially things that seem like a threat.

No, saber-toothed tigers are not lurking in middle school (unless it's your mascot), but there are *plenty* of things that may feel like threats and trigger judgment.

(Off-Topic) Scientific Fact about Saber-Toothed Tigers:

The saber-toothed tiger is also called the saber-toothed lion or saber-toothed cat. But actually, it's not a tiger, a lion, or even a close relative to Fluffy, your neighbor's cat. It belongs to an extinct subfamily of the cat (Felidae) called Machairodontinae. (Yikes! Try to pronounce that word!)

But back to our topic. Judgmental thoughts happen quickly and instinctually in our brains, especially when we're feeling insecure or threatened. What does that look like in middle school?

Examples of Judgment Shared by Middle Schoolers:

"Who you hang out with really matters. Every group has a label, like jocks, gamers, nerds, popular kids. Whether it's true or not, if you're in that group, you get that label."

"When I wear something my friend doesn't like, he says something mean, then he says he's 'just kidding.' But I know he's not."

"I used to be friends with some not-so-nice girls. When I'd hang out with them, I felt I had to be rude sometimes or they wouldn't like me."

"During lunch, my group looks at other tables and makes fun of kids, mostly for fun."

Yes, most of us judge others to some degree *inside our heads*. We think negative thoughts about people and make assumptions that may not be true. The thoughts are ideas bouncing around in our heads. We can choose to express these thoughts or ignore them.

Judgment becomes harsh, however, when these thoughts *leave our heads* and *are expressed in our words or our actions*. When we share negative thoughts with others in the form of criticism and gossip, we give them life.

Definition of harsh judgment:

The act of criticizing, making fun of, or condemning others

Synonyms: criticism, faultfinding, disapproval of others

Antonyms: acceptance, open-mindedness, Great Aunt Betty

Not fun stuff! Clearly, middle school (and the world) would be better without harsh judgment. So why does it happen so much? Here's what middle schoolers think.

Why Do Kids Judge Other Kids in Middle School?

"*People want to fit in with the popular group. They might say 'She's sooo weird' so they look better. Also, insecurity. Putting other people down so you feel better about yourself.*"

"*I think kids are doing this because they might be jealous or insecure about themselves.*"

"*People judge others sometimes because they are different.*"

In a nutshell, middle schoolers think kids judge other kids *to fit in, because they feel jealous or insecure,* and/or *because they fear difference.* Understanding this helps make harsh judgment directed at you a little less painful because *it's not really about you. It's about them.* (Hey, that could be a motivational T-shirt!)

Important:

Sometimes people think they are being judged when they actually are not. For example, you wear a new shirt to school, and someone stares and laughs. You assume she's laughing at you, but she's actually thinking about something funny that happened earlier. Oops! That's not judgment; that's jumping to conclusions.

You Choose the Ending: The Diversity Club

You've noticed that some kids at school don't seem to fit in. Some of these kids dress differently than others. Some are interested in things that other kids aren't into. Some seem really uncomfortable with the whole social scene.

Jaycee is one of these students. She excels in school, except for the social part. It's almost like she doesn't understand social rules. Jaycee has noticed that she's not the only one that doesn't fit in. This gives her an idea.

She decides to start a "Diversity Club." The club's motto is: All students are welcome and accepted for who they are, as they are.

Jaycee posts signs around the school and personally invites some kids to be part of the

club. For the first time in a long time, Jaycee seems excited about school.

News of the Diversity Club spreads. Soon, the whole school's talking about it, but not in the way Jaycee had hoped. Some kids snicker and whisper rude comments as she walks by. Others dare their friends to join the club as a joke.

When you sit down at your lunch table, the topic of conversation is the Diversity Club. Your friends are laughing at the kids that might participate. One friend dares another to eavesdrop on a club meeting and report back to the group. Your friends then turn to you and ask what you think about the Diversity Club.

You choose the ending. What do you do?

ENDING A:

You join in the fun. (Turn to page 17.)

ENDING B:

You change the topic of conversation to something else. (Turn to page 17.)

ENDING C:

You defend the Diversity Club and the kids that participate. (Turn to page 17.)

ENDING D (OPTIONAL):

(Don't like any of these endings? Add a new ending, then turn to page 18.)

_____

_____

_____

_____

_____

_____

_____

Antidotes from Middle Schoolers: How to Deal with Judgment

Luckily, like venomous snakebites and other toxins, harsh judgment can be remedied by an antidote. Middle schoolers shared the following antidotes. **Place a check mark** by the approaches that would best help you deal with judgment. Feel free to add another antidote too.

☐ "When you are being judged negatively for who your friends are or how you dress, it doesn't feel so good. My advice is just to tune it out. You don't have to listen to them. Just be yourself and stick with positive people who bring you up instead of down."

☐ "If other people judge you and you also judge yourself, you are practically letting other people push you around. If you hear things like 'You're so stupid,' it's normal to feel bad for a few seconds, but all you have to do is remind yourself, 'I'm not stupid; I'm smart.'"

☐ "Accept that everyone comes from different places and different homes, and in general, everyone has something unique about them. So just accept people for who they are."

☐ "Think before you talk behind someone's back because it could really hurt their feelings. If you're thinking something negative about an individual or a group, don't say it. You might not know the whole story."

☐ _____

_____

_____

_____

_____

You Choose the Ending: The Diversity Club (Cont.)

Your friends then turn to you and ask what you think about the Diversity Club.

You choose the ending: What do you do?

ENDING A:

You join in the fun. After all, Jaycee is sitting at the next table and won't hear you. You joke that your friend would be a perfect fit for the Diversity Club because nobody likes them. Then you start a game of Truth or Dare and dare your friend to attend a club meeting.

ENDING B:

You change the topic of conversation to something else. Making fun of the Diversity Club isn't how you want to spend your lunchtime. Instead of responding to the question, you ask your friends if they saw the big game last night. The conversation changes to impressive plays and amazing athletes.

ENDING C:

You defend the Diversity Club and the kids that participate. You sit up tall and say, "You know, I think the Diversity Club is a cool idea. Kids are harsh to each other in middle school. I think it's great that Jaycee's creating a more accepting club. It's a positive thing for our school." After an awkward silence, one of your friends laughs and suggests that you join the club. You smile and say, "Maybe I will," then you change the subject to the upcoming school dance.

ENDING D (OPTIONAL):

_____

_____

_____

_____

_____

_____

_____

Important Stuff to Remember about Harsh Judgment:

1. Judgmental thoughts are a normal first reaction when people *feel insecure or threatened* in some way. Since middle school isn't the most comfortable place in the world, judgment can grow like mold on stale bread.

2. People sometimes judge others because they are struggling themselves. Maybe they're trying to be "cool" or to fit in. Or perhaps they feel bad about themselves. *It's really not about you.* (There's that T-shirt again.)

3. When you notice you're thinking judgmental thoughts, *pause.* Try to catch yourself before you speak, text, or do any harm. You can't get those words back.

4. Do things you love to feel good about yourself (e.g., hobbies, spending time with pets, helping others). When you feel good about yourself, you're less interested in sharing judgmental thoughts with others.

The Final Word

We ALL have judgmental thoughts sometimes. And we ALL have the power to keep these thoughts to ourselves. Simply put, limiting judgmental conversations will make middle school a better place.

Challenge for Change:

Challenge 1: Can you avoid speaking judgmentally about anyone for an entire day? Instead, see if you can only talk positively about others. Or, if you don't have anything positive to say about someone, don't say anything at all. Notice what happens and how you feel.

Challenge 2: Find some friends to join the challenge and see if the group can go a whole day without harshly judging anyone. Notice what effect this has on your conversations.

Chapter 2:

Weird Behavior #2—
Changing Friendships

Let's get back to our research. Remember, this is not a test. All you have to do is answer three simple questions.

(This Is Still NOT a Test)
Research Questions:

	YES	NO
Is your best friend now a different person than in fourth grade?	☐	☐
Does the invitation list to your birthday party this year look different than it did a few years ago?	☐	☐
Do you have a friend (or former friend) that suddenly stopped hanging out with you?	☐	☐

If you answered YES to any of these questions, congratulations! You've experienced the changing world of friendships. Whatever happened to BFF or Best Friends *Forever*?! Maybe BFFN—Best Friends *For Now*—is more accurate in middle school.

Changing Friendships Under the Microscope: What's Really Going On

Yes, the friendship scene in middle school is *really* different from the scene in elementary school. The best word to describe middle school friendships is *change*. Personalities change, interests change, groups change, and even moods change all the time. It's no wonder that friendships are in a state of flux! And all of this change feels pretty unsettling when you're in the midst of it.

Experiment A: A (Not Very) Scientific Illustration of How Unsettling Change Feels

*Imagine you are entering the **candy store**. Mysterious aromas fill your nose. Luckily, you know exactly where to find your favorite **candy**, so you head straight there. But wait! It's not there. Where is it? You search everywhere, until finally,*

*you find the **candy** on the opposite side of the **candy store**. Oddly, it's surrounded by unfamiliar **candies**. And it's really different! What is happening? You begin to wonder if this is still your favorite **candy**.*

Experiment B:

[**WARNING**: This could trigger sweaty palms, an upset stomach, or nightmares. Take DEEP BREATHS and proceed with caution.]

Re-read Experiment A, replacing the following words:

Replace **candy store** with **lunchroom**. Replace **candy** with **friend**.

(Off-Topic) Facts about Candy:

Cotton candy is called "fairy floss" in Australia and "candy floss" in the United Kingdom. Did you know that December 7th is National Cotton Candy Day, April 12th is National Licorice Day, and May 23rd is National Taffy Day? Let the celebrations begin!

But back to our topic. Friendship changes are common in middle school. Kids even change what they are looking for in friendship and what qualities they are drawn to in friends.

Middle Schoolers
Describe the Friendship Scene:

"Friendships are all over the place. You are friends one day and not the next!"

"My group of friends pretty much dumped me last year, so I had to make new friends."

"Sometimes, I eat lunch in my classroom to avoid the whole lunch scene."

"We had a friend last year who was always in our group and was super nice, but this year they don't ever hang out with us. We have no idea why."

"Sometimes, friendship changes are good. I found people I really like and fit in with in middle school."

Why Are Friendship Changes in Middle School So Common?

"I think it's because kids really want to make new friends and to keep their options open."

"Some kids want to be 'cool' and be accepted into a more popular group, so they change friends."

"I think kids change friends because they may feel left out or like they don't really fit. So they try to find a more accepting group of friends."

"Sometimes, you are forced to find new friends because you get dumped by your group."

In a nutshell, middle schoolers think friends change groups for three main reasons:

1. To find new friends that feel like a good fit

2. To be part of a certain group or activity

3. Because they need or want a fresh start

From a scientific perspective, it's important to understand that humans share a fundamental need to feel *acceptance* and *belonging*. Early humans increased their chances of survival if they were part of a tribe, so our species evolved with the strong desire to be part of a group.

However, things get interesting (and weird) when we apply the human need for *acceptance* and *belonging* to middle school. Some kids try to fill this need by finding one or a few close friends. Others try to have tons of friends. Some try to draw attention to themselves by doing strange stuff. And others think that gaining popularity is the golden ticket. (Did that just describe the lunchroom scene or what?!)

You Choose the Ending: Best Friends Forever?

You've had pretty much the same group of friends for the past few years. You've shared a lot of great times, but lately, you've noticed that things aren't as fun as they used to be. Your interests are changing, so there's less to talk about and do together.

There are some other kids at school that you're excited to get to know. There's this one kid in your math class that you think is especially cool. You begin to wonder what it'd be like to hang out with a different group, but you have no idea how to make that change.

One morning, your old friends send a group text about hanging out together on Friday night. You reply that you'll be there.

Later that same day, that kid in your math class invites you to a birthday party on Friday night. You're psyched until you remember that you accepted another invitation for that same evening.

There's no way to do both.

You choose the ending: What do you do?

ENDING A:

You hang out with your old friends on Friday since you agreed to that first. (Turn to page 29.)

ENDING B:

You send a vague text to your old friends that you can no longer make it on Friday, and then you go to your new friend's birthday party. (Turn to page 29.)

ENDING C:

You go to your new friend's birthday party after explaining the situation to your old friends. (Turn to page 30.)

ENDING D (OPTIONAL):

(Don't like any of these endings? Add a new ending, then turn to page 30.)

_____

_____

_____

_____

_____

_____

_____

_____

_____

Antidotes from Middle Schoolers: How to Deal with Changing Friendships

Changing friendships can feel more stressful than taking a test you forgot to study for, so it's essential to have a way to deal. Middle schoolers shared the following antidotes. **Place a check mark** by the approaches that would best help you when you are in the midst of friendship changes. Feel free to add another antidote too.

☐ "Try not to worry. Good friendships are hard to find. You'll end up with a good set of friends by high school."

☐ "It's okay to have a variety of friends in several groups, so you always have a place where you feel accepted."

☐ "Be yourself and eventually, you will find the right group that likes you as you are. People continue to change, so try not to burn too many bridges since you'll be with the same kids through high school."

☐ "Be friendly. Put yourself out there. This way you will have a better chance of finding people you connect with."

☐ _____

_____

_____

_____

You Choose the Ending:
Best Friends Forever? (Cont.)

*Later that day, that kid in your math class invites you to
a birthday party on Friday night. You're psyched until you
remember that you accepted another invitation for that
same evening.*

There's no way to do both.

You choose the ending: What do you do?

ENDING A:

You hang out with your old friends on Friday since you
agreed to that first. You find yourself wishing you were
at the other party, but you quickly snap out of it and
have a great night. Later, you realize it's pretty awesome
to have a variety of friends to hang out with.

ENDING B:

You send a vague text to your old friends that you can
no longer make it on Friday,
and then you go to your new
friend's birthday party. You
don't explain why you can't
make it because it's really
none of their business.

♥ 15
B-DAY BOY!

Your new friend's birthday
party is amazing! Pictures
are posted on social media.

Your old friends see the photos and are mad that you ditched them for a "better" party. You feel embarrassed, so you avoid your old friends entirely and start hanging out with your new friend's group. Every time you pass one of your old friends in the hall, you feel uncomfortable.

ENDING C:

You go to your new friend's birthday party after explaining the situation to your old friends. It's totally awkward, but during lunch, you share that you are excited about going to the birthday party and doing that instead.

You have a blast at the party! The next week at school is a little weird with your old friends. They make some snide jokes about you and your "new friends." It's uncomfortable, but you just keep trying to be honest and open to new friendships.

ENDING D (OPTIONAL):

_____

_____

_____

_____

_____

_____

Important Stuff to Remember about Changing Friendships:

1. All friendships naturally change over time. But, like crushes, braces, and pimples, friendship changes are *especially common* in middle school.

2. There are *many reasons* why friendships change. Try not to take it personally. All you can really do is be the type of friend you would like to have.

3. It's hard when friendships end, but endings lead to *new beginnings* and *new friendships.*

The Final Word

Everyone looks for different things in friendship, but deep down, everyone is trying to find the same stuff: *acceptance and belonging.* Friendships change a lot in middle school. Try not to take it personally, and stay open to new friendships.

Challenge for Change:

Challenge 1: Your tribe is your vibe. Think about your current friends. Would you *describe* them as kind and respectful to you as well as to kids outside of your friend group? Which kids in your grade are genuinely kind and respectful to everyone?

Challenge 2: Have you ever changed friendships to gain more popularity? What did you gain and lose in the process?

Chapter 3:

Weird Behavior #3—
The Whole
"Popularity" Thing

Now, back to our research! Let's delve into the whole "popularity" thing. A word of warning: this scene gets really strange really fast. To start, please honestly answer three questions.

(This Is Not a Test)
Research Questions:

YES NO SOMETIMES

Are the "popular" kids in your grade widely liked by others in school? ☐ ☐ ☐

Do the "popular" kids tend to be kind and respected? ☐ ☐ ☐

Do you consider yourself one of the "popular" kids? ☐ ☐ ☐

If you answered NO or SOMETIMES to these questions, it sounds like you are dealing with the whole "popularity" thing. Simply put, popularity in middle school is an anomaly. (An "anomaly" is a fancy way of saying something is abnormal or peculiar.)

Examples of the Popularity Scene Shared by Middle Schoolers:

"For a while, I was part of a group of girls that were 'popular.' Then a couple of friends and I got sick of them because they were mean, so we stopped hanging out with them. We realized the only reason we hadn't moved away sooner was because we were scared about what they would say about us."

"In middle school, almost everyone cares about how popular they are, what they wear, who they like, and who likes them."

"I think that the popularity scene happens because everyone wants to be known by everybody."

"I call it 'popularitis,' which basically describes how some people change when they become popular and think they are better than others."

Middle schoolers report that some of the most popular kids are widely disliked, yet many kids secretly envy them. *Huh. What?!* Luckily, there's an explanation for this phenomenon.

Definition of popularity:

The state of being liked by many people.

Examples of popular things: Yoda, ice cream, and school holidays. (Okay, these aren't people, but you get the idea. Lots of people genuinely like these things.)

How Middle Schoolers Define Popularity:

"Popular girls are attractive, and the boys are athletic."

"Need to dress a certain way, date, and act a certain way to stay part of the group."

"Usually have money and the latest technology."

"Some popular kids act superior to others—don't let others in."

"Admired, but also feared."

Disclaimer:

Not every "popular" person in middle school behaves the same way. Some are well-liked students as described in Experiment P. This chapter explores the "popularity" that fits the middle school definition because it's, well . . . kind of fascinating.

Popularity Under the Microscope: What's Really Going On

When we compare the dictionary's definition of popularity with what actually happens in middle school, things get confusing. In middle school, "popularity" does not necessarily mean someone is well-liked or nice. Let's dissect this contradiction to understand what's going on. Slip on your lab coats!

Experiment P: A (Not Very) Scientific Dissection of Middle School "Popularity"

Let's pretend that the word "popular" no longer exists. Zap! It's erased from the dictionary. Now let's describe this middle school scene using different terms.

New Terms (Since "P" Word Now Extinct)	Definition	Typical Qualities
"Well-Liked" Students	the people everyone genuinely likes the most	• kind and cooperative • make others feel good about themselves • good listeners • handle conflict in healthy ways, usually not aggressive
"High-Status" Students	the people that strive for visibility and dominance	• combine kindness and meanness to enhance social status • may be socially or physically aggressive • drama-o-rama • may be feared by others

Hmmm . . . without the "P" word, a clearer view of the social scene emerges.

Interesting Fact about Middle School "Popularity":

Middle schoolers place more importance on popularity than younger kids or older teens. This is partly explained by what is happening in the adolescent brain. In adolescence, neurochemicals flood the mind, increasing the need to connect and bond with others. As a result, *attention from peers grows in importance.* As you may witness or experience, one way to get attention in middle school is through dominance, aggression, and power. Ta-da! "Popularitis" is born. Luckily, it's a temporary condition!

Good news! The middle school definition of popularity does not last long. By the middle of high school, most students align with the dictionary's definition. (Phew!)

Random Facts about Ice Cream:

Can you guess the most popular flavor of ice cream? According to the International Dairy Foods Association, vanilla is the number one flavor because it is so versatile. Think pie à la mode, root beer floats, and hot fudge sundaes. Chocolate holds the number two spot, followed by cookies and cream at number three. (Now we're talking!)

You Choose the Ending: Group Alliances

Your group of friends is considered one of the "popular" groups in school. You like the attention, but at times, the group can be sort of critical of others.

Lately, one of the kids in the group has been taking a lot of heat. A couple of your friends no longer like this person and are not shy about making them feel bad. You can tell they no longer want this person in the group.

You sometimes get annoyed by this kid too, but it's tough for you to watch this treatment. The teasing and backstabbing are relentless.

One day, the group plans a prank on this kid. They think it will be hilarious, but you know it will be humiliating and cruel.

You choose the ending: What do you do?

ENDING A:

You privately let the kid know what is about to happen. (Turn to page 41.)

ENDING B:

You confront the group and ask them not to do the prank. (Turn to page 41.)

ENDING C:

You start hanging out with another set of friends. (Turn to page 42.)

ENDING D (OPTIONAL):

(Don't like any of these endings? Add a new ending, then turn to page 43.)

_____

_____

_____

_____

_____

_____

Antidotes from Middle Schoolers: How to Deal with the Whole "Popularity" Thing

The "high-status" form of popularity, as described in Experiment P, is perplexing. Middle schoolers shared the following antidotes. **Place a check mark** by the approaches that would best help you navigate this scene. Feel free to add your own antidote.

☐ "Just go and find the kind of people that accept you for who you are."

☐ "Be careful about trying to fit in because you think it may improve your reputation. It may hurt you in the process."

☐ "People try to 'be cool' to be popular. I would say that it doesn't really matter if you are 'cool' as long as you have good friends."

☐ _____

_____

_____

_____

_____

_____

 ## You Choose the Ending: Group Alliances (Cont.)

One day, the group plans a prank on this kid. They think it will be hilarious, but you know it will be humiliating and cruel.

You choose the ending: What do you do?

ENDING A:

You privately let the kid know what is about to happen. You don't want to lose your place in the group, but you also don't want the prank to humiliate someone. The group figures out that you told and is not happy about it. Now you are the target of jokes and teasing. You start to think about joining a different group.

ENDING B:

You confront the group and ask them not to do the prank. You tell them that it's a bad idea and mean. One other friend sides with you, but the rest laugh it off and continue with the plan. You don't want to watch, so you leave. You later hear it was so humiliating, it brought the target to tears. You decide at that moment that you need some new friends.

ENDING C:

You start hanging out with another set of friends. You realize that your friends do not really act like friends. Your old group is not happy about your departure and starts some rumors about you. You're not surprised. It's uncomfortable for the first week or so, but then it gets better, and you are grateful to be hanging out with people that know how to treat others.

ENDING D (OPTIONAL):

_____

_____

_____

_____

_____

_____

Important Stuff to Remember about "Popularity" in Middle School:

1. "Popularity" in middle school doesn't necessarily mean a person is well-liked or nice. (Hmmm, that's weird.)

2. "Well-liked" people focus on kindness and cooperation. "High-status" people focus more on being dominant and the center of attention.

3. By the middle of high school, the definition of "popularity" aligns more with the dictionary. (Thankfully!)

The Final Word

In middle school, there's a difference between "popularity" and being well-liked. The qualities of well-liked students gain the respect of their peers.

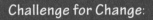

Challenge for Change:

Challenge 1: Review Experiment P. Do you have more qualities that align with "well-liked" students or "high-status" students?

Challenge 2: Think about a student that is "well-liked." What do you admire about them?

Chapter 4:

Weird Behavior #4— Crushes & Warp-Speed Dating

· ·

Now, the chapter you've been waiting for: crushes and dating. Like the whole "popularity" thing, the dating scene is puzzling. Not to mention awkward! Let's see if we can dissect what's going on and why. Safety goggles advised.

(This Is Not a Test) Research Questions:

	YES	NO
Have you experienced a racing heart or been completely tongue-tied when a certain person entered the room?	☐	☐
Did your thoughts wander back to this certain person over and over when you were supposed to be thinking about something else (like math)?	☐	☐

	YES	NO
If you learned that this certain person "liked" someone else, would you feel bummed?	☐	☐

If you answered YES to any of these questions, you likely have experienced a crush. If you answered NO to all of these, **do not worry**—rather, count yourself lucky! You have one less distraction in school. Everyone's on their own timeline when it comes to crushes. Some middle schoolers experience them, and others don't.

Origin of the word crush:

The word "crush" might come from the word "mash," which in 1870 was a popular way of saying you were "head over heels in love." Back then, to crush something was to mash it. So, where did "mash" come from? Mash referred to a "spoon-diet," which is linked to the word "spoony." In the 1820s, to be "spoony on someone" meant that you liked them. (Well, not sure that clears anything up!)

The (Not Very) Scientific Middle School Crush Scale

Big-time crushes!	Sometimes interested	Not sure	What's a crush again?

Definition of crush:

(Noun) An intense, but usually short-lived, infatuation for someone.

(Verb) To pulverize or compress forcefully.

Example: I felt crushed when my crush danced with someone else.

(Hmmm . . . maybe the term "crush" comes from crushed hearts?)

Having a crush is a fairly normal (yet intense) human experience. Some kids have one crush after another. This flowing stream of crushes becomes the focus of their conversations and thoughts. (How do they concentrate in school?!) Other kids couldn't care less.

It's not hard to imagine how two friends that fall on opposite ends of the Crush Scale might feel a strain in their conversations and possibly even their friendship. (See Chapter 2—"Changing Friendships.")

The mystery and intrigue of who has a crush on whom fuels an endless cycle of gossip and rumors in middle school. *AJ likes Jesse. No, wait! Actually, AJ likes Carson now. But Carson likes AJ's friend Jamie! Uh-oh.*

Most crushes are one-directional, dimming over time, or get replaced by a new crush. On rare occasions, two people have a crush on each other at the same time. (Fireworks!) This brings up the topic of dating. Someone NOT in middle school might assume that crushes lead to dating, but there's way more to the story. Let's dive deeper into understanding the dating scene.

Examples of the Dating Scene Shared by Middle Schoolers:

"Kids are 'dating,' but they don't even talk to each other. They just want to say they are dating."

"Kids date to seem mature and cool and to gain social status. Appearance and popularity drive dating."

"Kids you date need to be in your social rank or your friend groups."

"Some kids are into dating, but most actually are not."

"Kids would rather just hang out with friends instead of date, but they feel pressured."

"There may be a few couples that actually care about each other and stay together a while, but that's pretty rare."

Exhibit D: A (Not Very) Scientific Chart Comparing Adult vs. Middle School Dating

Typical Adult Dating Scene	Typical Middle School Dating Scene
Two people that are genuinely interested in getting to know each other.	Two people that have been encouraged by friends to date. They may or may not be interested in each other.
Go on dates and spend time together.	Hardly hang out. When they hang out, it's awkward.
Get to know each other.	Don't get to know each other well. Might rather be hanging out with friends.
Relationship may last for weeks, months, or more.	Relationship rarely lasts long (a.k.a. warp speed).
When the relationship ends, the couple meets face to face to discuss breaking up.	Breakups often happen via text, social media, or through a friend without discussion.

Dating Under the Microscope: What's Really Going On

As illustrated in Exhibit D, the adult dating scene is pretty different from the middle school scene. (Phew!) There are several reasons for this, including age, experience, and maturity level. But one of the most important differences is the reason *why* adults date versus *why* middle schoolers date.

Why do adults date? Companionship and attraction.

Why do middle schoolers date? Peer pressure, social status, attraction, and, occasionally, for companionship. *(See Chapter 3—"The Whole 'Popularity' Thing" and Chapter 9—"Peer Pressure.")*

> *"I didn't really like the guy but felt I needed to date him anyway. My friends really pushed me."*

> *"I dated this girl for a while, and we actually would hang out, but I missed my friends."*

> *"Dances would be much better if there was not this pressure. If somebody dances with someone, everyone then thinks they 'like' each other and begins to pester them about dating."*

A Word of Caution about Sexting:

Sexting is defined as sending nude photos or videos via mobile phone or the internet. For example, someone you like or are dating may ask you to send a nude photo of yourself to prove that you really "like" or trust them. Do not fall for this! Many of these photos are shared with others. Remember, NOTHING POSTED ONLINE IS EVER PRIVATE. Plus, in some cases, sharing underage nude photos or videos is illegal.

You Choose the Ending: The Crush Crisis

At a sleepover, you and your good friend discover you have a crush on the SAME person. At first, it's funny, but then it gets uncomfortable. The school dance is next week, and you have no idea what to do. What if your crush wants to dance with your friend instead of you? Or how would your friend handle it if you danced with your crush? Or what if your crush dances with someone else entirely? The dance is in six days.

You choose the ending: What do you do?

ENDING A:

You decide to ignore your feelings. You let go of your crush and let your friend keep it. It's not worth jeopardizing your friendship. (Turn to page 53.)

ENDING B:

You decide to see how the dance goes and let the crush choose. (Turn to page 54.)

ENDING C:

You both promise to keep it secret. If the crush asks either one of you to dance, you will say no. (Turn to page 54.)

ENDING D (OPTIONAL):

(Don't like these endings? Add a new ending, then turn to page 55.)

_____

_____

_____

_____

_____

Antidotes from Middle Schoolers: How to Deal with Crushes and Dating

The crushes and dating scene is packed with peer pressure, drama, and awkward moments. Middle schoolers shared the following antidotes to help navigate this daunting scene. **Place a check mark** by the approaches that would best help you. Feel free to add another antidote too.

☐ "Best not to tell anyone your crush unless you really trust them."

☐ "Relax. Wait until high school. Don't make anything a big deal. Dating in middle school is way too awkward. Don't feel forced to do it."

☐ "If you don't talk to someone or know them, don't date them. Don't break up using technology. Find the courage to talk face to face."

☐ "My parents don't allow me to date. To be honest, this gives me a good excuse to stay out of it."

☐ _____

_____

_____

 You Choose the Ending: The Crush Crisis (Cont.)

The dance is in six days.

You choose the ending: What do you do?

ENDING A:

You decide to ignore your feelings. You let go of your crush and tell your friend to keep it. It's not worth jeopardizing your friendship. You go to the dance with your friends and, soon, the crush is informed that your friend likes

them. You don't really want to watch them dance, so you head to the hall. Just then, the crush taps you on the shoulder and asks YOU to dance. You are stunned. You would like to say yes, but you see your friend across the room. Their tears help you find the right words to say "Thanks, but I better not," because you don't want to hurt a good friend.

ENDING B:

You decide to see how the dance goes and let the crush choose. The week of the dance, things get crazy. Word leaks out that both of you have the same crush. The crush is bombarded with questions about who they like more. Your friend starts to flirt with the crush, which makes your group of friends begin to take sides. The day of the dance, the crush reveals they don't like either of you. To be honest, you feel a huge sense of relief. You and your friend decide to skip the dance and have a sleepover instead to repair your friendship.

ENDING C:

You both promise to keep it secret. If the crush asks either one of you to dance, you agree to say no. But deep inside, you wonder if your friend will really say no if asked. You try not to think about it. The night of the dance arrives. You and your friend make a point to stay as far from the crush as possible. This actually becomes fun.

The crush asks another person to dance, which makes you both laugh and have an even better time. You feel lucky to have such a good friend.

ENDING D (OPTIONAL):

_____

_____

_____

_____

_____

_____

Important Stuff to Remember about Crushes and Dating:

1. Some kids experience crushes in middle school, and others don't. Both are perfectly normal. (Although the latter person may experience fewer daydreams and distractions!)

2. The middle school dating scene is driven by *peer pressure, social status,* and *attraction* more than *companionship.* (No wonder it's so awkward!)

3. You do not have an obligation to have a crush or to go out with anyone because your friends want you to.

The Final Word

Everyone's on their own timeline when it comes to crushes. If you decide to enter the world of crushes, find friends that you trust so you can share your feelings and know those feelings will be respected.

Challenge for Change:

Challenge 1: Have you ever felt pressured into a crush or dating? How did that feel? For the next week, encourage your friends to make their own choices instead of being influenced by peer pressure.

Challenge 2: If you decide to date someone, speak in person (not via text or social media) when having difficult conversations, such as disagreements and breakups. Texts and messages are easily misunderstood or shared with others.

Chapter 5:

Weird Behavior #5—
The Ins and Outs of
Cliques & Groups

· ·

Wolves fight to determine alpha males and females. Primates establish social rankings with clear leaders and followers. Sometimes humans even demonstrate these tendencies, especially in middle school. (Surprise, surprise.) Let's dive into the science of group behavior.

(This Is Not a Test)
Research Questions:

	YES	NO
Have you ever been part of a group of friends that didn't want others to join?	☐	☐
Have you ever wanted to be part of a group but felt that you couldn't?	☐	☐

YES   NO

Have you ever thought you needed to act, speak, or dress a certain way to fit in with a group? ☐   ☐

If you answered YES to any of these, you have felt the impact of social cliques or groups. Cliques and middle school are like pancakes and syrup. It's hard to imagine one without the other.

Like many of the topics in this book, group behavior gets interesting when sliced open and studied. Let's clarify some definitions to start.

Definition of clique:

A small, exclusive group of people.

Definition of group:

A set of people who have the same interests or aims.

Clarification:

"Group" and "clique" have different definitions but are often used interchangeably with various meanings in middle school. For simplicity, both will be used to describe group behavior in this chapter.

Examples of the Group Scene Shared by Middle Schoolers:

"Some groups own certain tables in the lunchroom. Others wouldn't dare sit there."

"There are lots of private clubs, secret handshakes, and inside jokes. It's so uncomfortable when you are left out of this."

"Rude comments and dirty looks let kids know they don't belong in certain groups. My group tries not to be exclusive. We would rather it be just us, but we don't make others feel bad if they sit with us."

"Some groups are exclusive and non-accepting of others. They are filled with peer pressure to stay in the group and keep that status."

Origin of the Word "Clique":

Why are groups of people sometimes called cliques? The term "clique" originated in France in the 1700s and meant to latch or bolt a door. The word later evolved to describe tight-knit groups of people. Hmmm . . . no wonder joining a group sometimes feels like trying to open a locked door!

Chapter 5

Groups Under the Microscope: What's Really Going On

There's nothing wrong with being part of a group. Humans are social, so it's no surprise that people band together. In fact, many important human achievements, like the civil rights movement, are inspired by groups. But group behavior can also create a sense of division.

As discussed in Chapter 2—"Changing Friendships," humans share the universal need to be accepted and belong. It feels good to be part of something. Plus, it's fun to hang out with people that share your interests. *So, how might groups behave in a perfect world?* Let's take a field trip to United Unicorns Middle School.

Exhibit A: Group Behavior at United Unicorns Middle School
• All students have an *accepting* group of friends.
• All students and groups treat others well.
• All students regularly gather to hold hands and sing "Kumbaya." (Okay, maybe this last one is going a little too far, even for U.U.M.S!)

Chances are, you do not attend United Unicorns Middle School. This would be a short and lovely chapter if life were that simple. Group behavior in middle school is more complicated. Let's visit a typical middle school.

Exhibit B: Group Behavior in a Typical Middle School
• Some students have *accepting* friends, some have *unaccepting* friends, and some have *no group* and *few friends*.
• Some students and groups treat others well; in other groups, some kids *hold more power* and/or are *unkind*.
• *Acceptance, power,* and *what is "cool"* is always changing.
• Groups fall into a *rank* that ranges from "popular" to "outcasts."

Fact about the Group Behavior of Chickens:

The term "pecking order" comes from the social hierarchy of chickens. Chickens of lower rank have fewer feathers because they have been pecked on by higher-ranking, aggressive chickens. Life in a chicken coop is definitely no picnic!

Why Do Kids Form Groups in Middle School?

"Similar interests. Same classes. Similar personalities. To fit in. To separate us versus them."

"I think it's partly because people are insecure about themselves, so they just want a group that they don't have to be judged by."

*"Popular boys only date popular girls, so some
kids try to get in those groups to be part of that
scene. These groups get a lot of attention too,
which some kids crave."*

**"I think kids are doing this because they have
certain interests. For example, some kids play
sports like basketball and football. Sometimes,
other kids want to join, but they are not as good
at sports."**

In a nutshell, middle schoolers think kids band together
because they *share interests, want to belong, want social
status, and/or to separate themselves from others.*
Because of the strong desire to "fit in," groups take
on a powerful role. This creates a "pecking order" or a
social ranking with some groups at the top while others
hover around the middle or bottom. Some students and
groups are "in," and others are "out." And the whole scene
is always changing.

Ideally (and in United Unicorns Middle School), school
is *a shared space of equals.* In reality (and in typical middle
schools), group behavior ends up making *many students
feel less than others.*

*So, what would make the middle school group scene less
of a pecking order? What would help kids treat others in
and out of their group better? What would make the typical*

middle school a teeny bit more like United Unicorns Middle School? The answer is **dignity**.

Definition of dignity:

The recognition that all people have value and worth.

All humans share a deep desire to be treated as something of value. Everyone wants to be seen, heard, listened to, and treated fairly. Dignity is the opposite of the chicken coop's pecking order. See Exhibit C.

Exhibit C: Middle School Examples of Treating Others with Dignity
• "Saving inside jokes, secret handshakes, and private club/group meetings for times when those not involved are not around."
• "Not whispering to someone in front of others."
• "Not ranking people on scales of coolness or appearance."
• "Avoiding name-calling, judging, and labeling others."
• "Allowing people to be themselves and accepting differences."
• "It's possible to disagree and even dislike someone and still treat them with dignity."

Caution:

Even if your entire school read this book three times, you would still see kids disrespecting others. Treating others with dignity requires a lot of attention, kindness, and maturity. And mistakes are inevitable. Heck, many adults struggle with this! Hang in there. Over time, the words and actions of a few leaders can shift group behavior for the better.

You Choose the Ending: New Addition to the Group

After a rocky start to middle school, you've finally settled in to a good group of friends. They're really nice, avoid drama, and accept you for who you are. It feels great to be part of this group, and you look forward to meeting up at lunch every day.

One day, a new person begins to sit with you and your group. You're not happy about this because this person sometimes says rude things. But since your group tries to be accepting, you welcome them in.

After a few days, the group dynamic begins to change. The new friend likes to embarrass people and make snide comments about what people say and do. They say they're "just joking," but it doesn't feel like a joke. This is creating a negative vibe at your table,

and the group is getting frustrated. Instead of looking forward to lunch, you begin to dread it.

One afternoon, the new friend says something that makes one of your friends so mad, they leave the lunch table and sit with a different group. You're really concerned that your friend group is going to break up.

You choose the ending: What do you do?

ENDING A:

You tell this person not to sit with you anymore. (Turn to page 67.)

ENDING B:

You and your friends make a plan to avoid this person at lunch. (Turn to page 67.)

ENDING C:

You let the new friend know how your group treats one another. (Turn to page 68.)

ENDING D (OPTIONAL):

(Don't like these endings? Add a new ending, then turn to page 68.)

_____

_____

_____

_____

_____

_____

Antidotes from Middle Schoolers: How to Deal with Cliques and Groups

Friendships change a bunch in middle school, which means groups change too. At some point, everyone experiences changes in their social circles. The following antidotes were shared by middle schoolers to help navigate this scene. **Place a check mark** by the approaches that would best help you. Feel free to add another antidote too.

☐ "If you want to join a certain group, first make friends with a few people in the group."

☐ "If your friend is in a group that you are not in, don't take it personally. If you feel excluded, go find friends that share your interests and like you for who you are."

☐ "In sixth grade, it took me a while to find friends. When I needed a break from the lunchroom, my science teacher always let me eat lunch in her classroom. This really helped."

☐ "Find a group of friends that's similar to you and make sure you trust them. Even though you have your group, be kind to everyone else."

☐ _____

_____

_____

You Choose the Ending:
New Addition to the Group (Cont.)

*One afternoon, the new friend says something that makes
one of your friends so mad, they leave the lunch table and
sit with a different group. You're really concerned that your
friend group is going to break up.*

You choose the ending: What do you do?

ENDING A:

   You tell this person not to sit with you anymore. After
lunch, you and your friends gather and agree this person
is ruining your group. You offer to tell the new addition
that the group doesn't want them to join at lunch. You're
nervous to say this, so you decide to send a text that
reads: *U really hurt someone's feelings today. Please do
not sit with us at lunch.* You hit send and feel great for a
moment. But then a pit forms in your stomach.

   The next day, your group sits together. Everyone
feels a little awkward and keeps looking around to see
where the person is sitting. You still have a pit in your
stomach and wish that you'd handled the situation a
different way.

ENDING B:

   You and your friends make a plan to avoid this person
at lunch. You secretly decide to eat in a classroom for a
few days. That afternoon in class, the new addition asks

where everyone was at lunch. You shrug your shoulders because you don't know what to say. The next day, the group eats in the classroom again. It becomes clear to the new addition that the group is avoiding them. You can see they are really sad about this. You begin to wonder if there was a better way to handle this.

ENDING C:

You let the new friend know how your group treats one another. The next day at lunch, when they start to embarrass someone, you ask them to stop. Then you calmly say, "I like having you sit with us, but it's important for you to know that our group tries really hard to be respectful of each other and not make others feel bad." The new addition looks surprised, but nods and says, "Okay." The rest of the lunch period actually goes pretty well. You realize you may need to remind the new friend about this again but feel good that some boundaries have been put in place.

ENDING D (OPTIONAL):

_____

_____

_____

_____

_____

_____

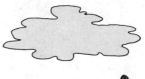

Important Stuff to Remember about Cliques and Groups:

1. Sometimes it takes a while to find friends that feel like a good fit. (And, of course, no friend group is ever perfect!)

2. Group behavior gets ugly when a person or group behaves (or pecks) in a way that makes others feel less worthy. (Luckily, humans don't have beaks. Ouch!)

3. Treating others with dignity will significantly improve the social scene.

The Final Word

It's natural to have a group of friends you prefer, but be sure to treat others well too. Treating others with dignity is possible, even in middle school.

 **Challenge for Change**:

Challenge 1: Do you and your friends have inside jokes or clubs that are private to your group? For the next week, do not talk about these when others are around. Save these conversations for times when others will not feel excluded.

Challenge 2: Think about someone in your school that treats others with dignity. What does this person do to make sure others feel worthy and respected?

Chapter 6:

Weird Behavior #6— Gossip & Drama-O-Rama

• •

You are the next contestant in the game *Gossip or Not Gossip*. (Wild applause!) Read the scenarios below and choose whether you think it's gossip or not. Good luck!

A friend shares the secrets of other friends with you and asks you not to tell.

GOSSIP   NOT GOSSIP

☐   ☐

You complain to a friend about a kid in your class that's really annoying. Your friend nods in agreement and adds more annoying stories about this person.

GOSSIP   NOT GOSSIP

☐   ☐

The lunchroom buzzes with news about a kid that got suspended.

GOSSIP   NOT GOSSIP

☐   ☐

If you selected that *all of the above* are gossip, congratulations! You are correct and the winner of a shiny new dishwasher. Most people gossip, whether they admit it or not. And, like a pesky cold, gossip is especially contagious in middle school.

Definition of gossip:

(Noun) Conversation about other people that might be unkind, disapproving, or untrue.

Examples of Gossip
Shared by Middle Schoolers:

"Gossip can be like a game of telephone. The story changes over time."

"I'd heard that one of my good friends told people that I did something I hadn't. It turns out it was a big misunderstanding, but it caused a lot of drama and hurt feelings."

"One of my friends called my other friend a bunch of stuff behind her back. This completely divided our group. They both avoided each other for a while until the person who said everything finally told my friend that she wanted to be friends again. They were friends until she did it again a little while later."

Disclaimer:

Okay, there may be a student or two that's completed Jedi training and does not gossip. But pretty much the rest of us do until we begin our own Jedi training.

Gossip Under the Microscope: What's Really Going On

Why is gossip so common in middle school? To start, let's dissect different types of gossip. Lab coats!

Types of Gossip	Middle School Examples	Why Kids Gossip about This
TYPE 1: News about others' behaviors or activities	Suspensions, fights, new and different behaviors *"Did you hear what happened to Jake?"*	• To understand what is going on with other kids in school (who's doing what, what's in/out or cool/uncool)
TYPE 2: Sharing secrets and private information about others	Crushes, embarrassing stories, rumors *"OMG! You won't believe what Liv just told me . . ."*	• Social climbing or insecurity (putting others down to feel better about self or to gain status) • Entertainment
TYPE 3: Sharing complaints or criticism about others	Who's stuck up, selfish, mean, annoying, bossy, lying, teacher's pet, fake, uncool, etc. *"She's so fake. She'll say anything to try to be cool."*	• Social climbing or insecurity (putting others down to feel better about self or to gain status) • Fear of conflict (talking to others instead of directly to the person involved)

(Off-Topic) About Jedi Training:

If you've never seen the movie *Star Wars*, you might not know about Jedi training. Basically, young warriors learn to use "the Force" to fight for good. With the help of a tiny green man and loads of practice, Jedis learn cool mind tricks to defeat evil. It sounds a little weird, but it's powerful stuff that saves the entire universe from doom and gloom.

But back to our topic. Gossip comes in many flavors, but *three key ingredients* make it especially toxic. See Exhibit G: What Makes Gossip Toxic? Safety goggles advised.

Exhibit G: What Makes Gossip Toxic?

> **GOSSIP: Three Toxic Ingredients**
> **(Caution! This is where gossip gets ugly.)**
>
> 1. Gossip is laced with **harsh judgment** (see Chapter 1)
>
> 2. Gossip is **one sided** (only one story or opinion shared)
>
> 3. Gossiper **talks to others instead of directly to person involved** (a.k.a. behind their back)
>
> **The (not very) scientific formula for drama-o-rama:**
> Gossip + Harsh Judgment+ One sided+
> Behind their Back = D-R-A-M-A (or G+HJ+1+BB = DRAMA)

Raise your hand if you like drama. That's what I thought. Not fun stuff! Hmmm . . . so why is it so common?

Why Do Kids Gossip in Middle School?

"I think kids are doing this because they don't like the person they spread rumors about."

"Kids do this because they want to get attention, or they do it because they want to hurt the other person."

"Some kids have really different personalities, so they clash. Instead of dealing with each other, they gossip to take each other down. Then other kids take sides, which makes things worse."

"Nobody wants to be the last one to know the latest gossip. This makes it important to stay in the loop."

"I think that kids are doing it to stay entertained. They don't know what else to talk about."

In a nutshell, middle schoolers think kids gossip for *entertainment, attention, to belong,* or *because they don't like someone.* Yuck! When spelled out in black and white, gossip becomes much less attractive.

You Choose the Ending: The Center of the Storm

You are ready for a fresh start. Some of your old friends are going in different directions, and you want a change too. A few weeks into the school year, you find some new friends you really connect with, so you start spending more time with them.

One of your old friends is upset that you changed groups. You hear from others that they are calling you things like "loser" and "traitor." This bothers you, but you decide to let it go. Maybe it will stop.

Instead, it gets worse. Your old friend shares an embarrassing story about you in class. The story quickly spreads. You feel angry and betrayed. But most of all, you want this to stop.

You choose the ending: What do you do?

ENDING A:

You send a text message to your old friend, warning them to stop. (Turn to page 78.)

ENDING B:

You confront your old friend when you are alone in the hall. (Turn to page 79.)

ENDING C:

You gather your new friends and confront your old friend as a group. (Turn to page 80.)

ENDING D (OPTIONAL):

(Don't like these endings? Add a new ending, then turn to page 80.)

_____

_____

_____

_____

_____

_____

Antidotes from Middle Schoolers: How to Deal with Gossip and Drama

Gossip, plus the toxic ingredients (see Exhibit G), fills the halls of middle school with drama. But, with some Jedi training, it's possible to not participate in this scene. Middle schoolers shared the following antidotes. **Place a check mark** by the approaches that would best help you extinguish the flames of gossip. Feel free to add another antidote too.

☐ "Don't listen to gossip. Instead, talk to the person whom the gossip is about."

☐ "Pretend that whoever you are talking about is right next to you. Only say things you would be okay with them hearing."

☐ "Don't pick sides. You don't know the whole story."

☐ "You are most likely to be similar to the friends you are around the most. Hang out with the people who avoid drama, are nice, and are easygoing."

☐ _____
_____
_____

You Choose the Ending: The Center of the Storm (Cont.)

Instead, it gets worse. Your old friend shares an embarrassing story about you in class. The story quickly spreads. You feel angry and betrayed. But most of all, you want this to stop.

You choose the ending: What do you do?

ENDING A:

You send a text message to your old friend, warning them to stop. You write, *I know what u r saying about me. u better STOP. y r u even doing this?* You send the message and wait. A while later, you get a text back.

W/E. . . .y r u such a traitor? What r u gonna do about it anyway? LOL. Your heart sinks. You decide not to get into a back-and-forth text argument and begin to think about another way to deal with this.

ENDING B:

You confront your old friend when you are alone in the hall. Since all you have to go on is rumors, you decide not to jump to conclusions. You say, "Hey, can I talk to you for a second? I've heard from a few people that you have been calling me things like "traitor" and "loser." I also heard that you shared an embarrassing story about me with your class. What's going on?"

Your old friend looks uncomfortable, but you hold your gaze and stand your ground. Eventually, your friend says, "Whatever. I don't even know what you're talking about."

You reply, "Well, if it's true, I don't like it. Next time you have something to say about me, find the courage to say it directly to me." Then you walk off. You're not sure it will help, but you're glad you kept your cool and took the higher ground.

ENDING C:

You gather your new friends and confront your old friend as a group. When your old friend goes to the lockers after school, you and your group are waiting. With a shove, you tell your old friend to stop talking behind your back. Your group adds a few insults. Then you walk off.

The next day, you are in for a surprise. As you close your locker, you feel a group gather around you. Your old friend and a few other kids push you against the wall and warn you never to gang up on them again. A teacher hears the commotion, and all of you end up in the principal's office.

ENDING D (OPTIONAL):

_____

_____

_____

_____

_____

_____

_____

Important Stuff to Remember about Gossip:

1. Gossip is common in middle school and is a regular cause of conflict and drama. (The lunchroom would be a much quieter place without it!)

2. When we understand the reasons why we gossip, it makes it *much less* attractive.

3. Like harsh judgment, gossip can be reduced or stopped when we choose not to share critical thoughts and personal information about others.

The Final Word

When you are about to begin gossiping, STOP. Instead, find the courage to speak directly to the person you have a conflict with or remain silent. Talk about others the way you would want them to talk about you. (Jedi training in action!)

Challenge for Change:

Challenge 1: Can you go an entire day without sharing criticisms or secrets about others? Give it a try and notice the effect this has on you, your feelings, your conversations, and your friendships.

Challenge 2: Begin a week-long contest with your family. Whenever someone gossips, the gossiper adds some money to a jar. At the end of the week, the person that gossiped the least wins the money. Notice what the gossip ban does to your conversations.

Chapter 7:

Weird Behavior #7— Social Media, Phubbing, & FOMO

• •

Whether it's Instagram, Snapchat, TikTok, or the latest, greatest app, social media is a BIG part of many middle schoolers' lives. (Which is quite amazing, actually, since most of these apps restrict users under the age of 13. Hmmm?) But anyway, there are awesome things about social media and, of course, there's not-so-awesome stuff too. Let's start with some research.

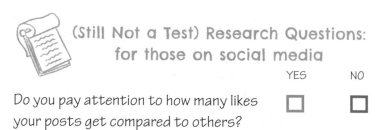

(Still Not a Test) Research Questions: for those on social media

	YES	NO
Do you pay attention to how many likes your posts get compared to others?	☐	☐

	YES	NO

Have you ever felt bummed after check-ing social media and seeing that your friends got together without you? ☐ ☐

Have you ever seen or heard of someone sharing a photo or post about another person they shouldn't have? ☐ ☐

If you answered YES to any of these questions, you've experienced the not-so-great side of social media. Social media apps are designed to help people connect, but there are downsides. Let's dive in.

Social Media Under the Microscope: What's Really Going On

A recent study by Common Sense Media found that teens spend an average of seven hours every day on screens playing games, watching videos, and scanning social media. Wow! That's 106 days a year, not including any screen time spent on schoolwork. Girls usually spend more time on social media, while guys tend to spend more time gaming.

Random Thought:

Imagine if instead of averaging seven hours a day on screens, teens spent half of this time practicing something else they enjoy (learning to play an instrument, creating art, writing songs or books, mastering a sport, etc.). With that level of practice, there would be a lot more musicians, artists, writers, and athletes in the world!

What is it about social media that makes it so popular in middle school? Well, like friendships and groups, social media feeds the human need for *attention* and *belonging*. Since many middle schoolers have a phone, social media's an easy way to try to meet these needs.

"Everything in middle school is on social media. Most students have an account or two or three." (8th Grade Student)

Thoughts about Social Media Shared by Middle Schoolers:

"It's a way for everyone to stay in touch, but we measure ourselves on likes."

"When I hang out with my friends, they are all sucked in to their phones."

"Social media is a good way to communicate, but people also get superglued to it. I also feel like it's an easy way for people to make you feel bad about yourself."

"Social media helps you communicate with people, but it also makes you wish you are doing what others are doing or have what others have."

"It's really easy just to scroll and scroll on my phone to pass the time when I could be doing better things."

A Beginner's Guide to Social Media Apps & Posts:
Twitter: I'm eating a #cookie
Instagram: Here's a vintage photo of my cookie
TikTok or YouTube: Watch me eat my cookie
Pinterest: Here's my cookie recipe

Middle schoolers report that social media has both a positive and a negative side. To better understand this, see Exhibit S.

Exhibit S: Cool Versus Not-So-Cool Things about Social Media

Cool Things about Social Media	Not-So-Cool Things about Social Media
• Connect with and support friends	• Social comparison: *using likes and followers as a measure of self-worth*
• Be part of a larger community	• FOMO (Fear Of Missing Out): *seeing activities you weren't included in and feeling like you need to be on social media often, so you don't miss something*
• Follow inspiring people that are doing great things in the world	• Creates unrealistic expectations: *about beauty, relationships, and life*
• Learn about cool stuff and new things	• Cyberbullying: *using social media to put down, threaten, or harm others*

Many things in life are a mix of good and bad. Candy and cookie dough are delicious until you eat so much that you feel sick. Social media helps you connect with people, but it can also make you feel left out, lonely, and bad about yourself. The formula below helps to keep social media use positive.

The (Not So) Scientific Formula for Social Media Use So That Positives > Negatives
DO use social media to: • Connect with and encourage others • Explore your interests and goals • Make the world a better place • Follow inspiring people that are making positive changes in the world
DON'T use social media to: • Make fun of or humiliate others • Measure your self-worth or appearance • Post videos or photos of others without consent • Post things you want to keep private (Nothing posted online is ever private!) • Make the world a meaner place
Steps to Build Healthy Screen Time Habits • Set a daily screen time limit and monitor usage • Do not keep devices in your bedroom at night; put on "sleep mode" so your sleep is not disturbed (Seriously! Sleep is important, especially in middle school. No, your parents didn't ask to have that included in this book.) • Balance daily screen time with offline time hanging out with friends, getting outside, doing hobbies, etc.

Weird Fact:

Ever heard of nomophobia? It is the fear of being without your cell phone or losing your signal. Symptoms include increased heart rate, shortness of breath, anxiety, nausea, trembling, dizziness, depression, fear, or panic. Not surprisingly, this condition is on the rise among students. What's the cure? Turn your phone off for a while several times a day, spend plenty of time off screens each day, have a tech-free day at least once a month, and do not sleep with your phone nearby. (If these cures trigger panic, hmmm, maybe you are experiencing the beginning stages of nomophobia?)

You Choose the Ending: Quest for Followers

You recently joined a new social media app that everyone is talking about. In the first week, you gain over a hundred followers! Some are friends, and others are kids you don't know well. You post some pictures and notice how many likes you get. The positive response feels great until you see that some kids have a ton more followers and likes than you.

You decide you need to grow your following. You start to spend a lot more time on the app, reaching out to people and posting things you think others will like. Your following starts to improve but is still below many of your classmates.

You choose the ending: What do you do?

ENDING A:

You up your game and keep trying to grow your following. (Turn to page 91.)

ENDING B:

You turn off the app's notifications and try to stop worrying about it. (Turn to page 92.)

ENDING C:

You decide to use the app in a different way and follow only friends and people that inspire you. (Turn to page 92.)

ENDING D (OPTIONAL):

(Don't like these endings? Add a new ending, then turn to page 93.)

_____

_____

_____

_____

Antidotes from Middle Schoolers: Social Media Use

Social media can be a fun way to connect with others, but it has downsides. Middle schoolers shared the following antidotes to keep social media use positive. **Place a check mark** by the approaches that would best help you. Feel free to add another antidote too.

☐ "Post appropriate stuff, and don't worry about likes or what others think."

☐ "Be cautious about what you post. Nothing is private. Remember, your grandma, your principal, and even your future college might see your posts."

☐ "Just post things that make you and others happy, and follow your friends."

☐ "Understand you don't see the whole story. People only post the stuff they want you to see. Everyone has problems of their own."

☐ _____
_____
_____
_____
_____
_____
_____

Random Fact:

Merriam-Webster is watching a new term for possible inclusion in the dictionary. Ever heard of the word "phubbing?" It's the words "phone" and "snubbing" spliced together and refers to being snubbed by someone using a cell phone. For example, you are talking to your friend, and your friend keeps glancing at their phone. Or worse, your friend ignores you and focuses only on their phone. Yuck!

You Choose the Ending: Quest for Followers (Cont.)

You decide you need to grow your following. You start to spend a lot more time on the app, reaching out to people and posting things you think others will like. Your following starts to improve but is still below many of your classmates.

You choose the ending: What do you do?

ENDING A:

You up your game and keep trying to grow your following. You've only been on the app a few weeks, after all. With more time and effort, maybe you can gain hundreds of followers. You spend more time posting photos, liking posts, and finding people to follow. Perhaps they will then follow you. You carefully watch as your followers continue to grow. You start having a hard time keeping up with the long feed that now includes many people you don't even know.

You begin staying up late to keep up with posts and wonder if all of this time and effort is worth it.

ENDING B:

You turn off the app's notifications and try to stop worrying about it. You realize that you have been a little obsessed with gaining followers the past few weeks. You hope that by turning off notifications, you will not be so sucked into the app. You make an effort to get together with friends more often and only check the site a couple of times a day. It still feels a little weird that you don't have as many followers as others, but you try not to think about it. You know that has nothing to do with who you are as a person.

ENDING C:

You decide to use the app in a different way and follow only friends and people that inspire you. You go through the list of people you follow and scale back to only people you really know. Then, you start to follow some inspiring people that are doing amazing things in the world. You also begin to follow things related to your hobbies and interests. You notice that you are spending more time offline doing your hobbies. What you are seeing and learning is inspiring you to make the world a better place too.

ENDING D (OPTIONAL):

_____

_____

_____

_____

_____

_____

_____

Important Stuff to Remember about Social Media:

1. Social media has both positive and negative effects. (FOMO, nomophobia, and phubbing fall on the negative side!)

2. Using social media as a tool to connect and spread kindness helps to minimize the negatives. (#kindness)

3. Pay attention to how social media affects how you feel and modify screen habits as needed. (Since you are the first generation to grow up on screens, you are sort of guinea pigs in a global science experiment. Luckily, you have the power to change your habits!)

Chapter 7

The Final Word

Social media serves some, but not all, social needs. Use social media to spread goodwill and balance screen time with plenty of time offline doing things you enjoy.

Challenge for Change:

Challenge 1: This week, track how much time you spend on social media or screens. Do you think that's the right amount of time for you? If not, how would you change your habits? Try this new habit for the next week.

Challenge 2: If you are on social media, review the list of people you follow. Are you following some inspiring people that are making the world better? Are you following anyone that brings you down? Modify your list, and over the next week notice the impact this change has on your mood and your thoughts.

Chapter 8:

Weird Behavior #8– Conflict and Aggressive Behaviors . . . Ouch!

Middle schoolers tend to treat other students in positive or neutral ways, but there's no shortage of mean behaviors. And although schools work to prevent bullying, it still happens. Yuck! All of this adds up to painful feelings, conflict, and drama. To understand what's going on, let's start with a pop quiz. *(No peeking at the answers!)*

Pop Quiz: Is It Rude, Mean, or Bullying?

Question 1. Jake tells Marco that he can't play basketball after school because Marco's the worst player in 7th grade.

RUDE	MEAN	BULLYING
☐	☐	☐

Question 2. Molly makes fun of Penny a lot for wearing the same pants to school every day. Molly tells Penny that she smells in gym class, and later that week, she writes *You stink* on Penny's locker.

RUDE	MEAN	BULLYING
☐	☐	☐

Question 3. Alex had a party and didn't invite Kai. Kai thinks that Alex invited almost everyone else in their group.

RUDE	MEAN	BULLYING
☐	☐	☐

Hmmm. Without more information, it's tricky to know for sure what's going on in these situations. Signe Whitson is an internationally recognized author, speaker, and counselor that has worked with students for decades. In her book *8 Keys to End Bullying*, she shares definitions to help kids and schools better understand behaviors. Let's explore these definitions to clear things up a bit.

Definition of rude behavior:

Inadvertently saying or doing something that hurts someone else.

Definition of mean behavior:

Purposefully saying or doing something to hurt someone once or maybe twice.

Definition of bullying behavior:

Intentionally aggressive behavior, repeated over time, that involves an imbalance of power.

Pop Quiz Answers:

Question 1: It appears that Jake is being mean. He intended to hurt Marco with his words, but there's no evidence of bullying, such as repetitive behavior and a power imbalance. There's possibly an ongoing conflict between Jake and Marco. More information necessary.

Question 2: Molly's behaving like a bully. She's repeatedly making fun of Penny with harmful intention. There's also evidence of a power imbalance. There may be additional factors involved, such as an ongoing conflict. More information and intervention necessary.

Question 3: Since it is unclear whether Alex intentionally or unintentionally excluded Kai, it's difficult to determine whether this was mean or rude behavior. There also may be other factors involved, such as an ongoing conflict, Alex's parents limiting the number of party attendees, or changing friendship dynamics (see Chapter 2—"Changing Friendships.") More information necessary.

How did you do on the quiz? There's often a lot more to situations than first meets the eye. It's easy to jump to conclusions, make assumptions, and not consider the whole story. Some schools have moved away from labeling behaviors. Instead, these schools work directly with the students involved to resolve conflict. So yeah, the pop quiz needs another answer option: **More information necessary**.

To *really* understand what's happening, context is needed. Regardless, all of these situations are difficult. *So why does this sort of stuff happen so much in middle school?* Luckily, you've read Chapters 1–7, so this starts to make sense! See Exhibit Z.

Exhibit Z: An (Oversimplified) Illustration of the Impact of Some Middle School Experiences

Middle school experiences
such as changing friendships, new identities and interests, social climbing, crushes, cliques & groups, and gossip

↓

contribute to conflict, misunderstandings, and mistakes

↓

leading to CHANGE
personal growth, lessons learned, new skills, new relationships, etc.

Important: Exhibit Z illustrates some tricky middle school experiences, but there's positive stuff too! Think about the kindness, generosity, leadership, and courage you have experienced or witnessed. Because of the human tendency to remember negative stuff more than positive stuff, a.k.a. negativity bias, sometimes positive moments are quickly forgotten. See Chapter 11 for reminders of the good stuff!

Essentially, middle school is boot camp for navigating new experiences, new behaviors, and change. (Lucky you!) Many of these behaviors weren't around in elementary school, so middle schoolers learn on the fly. No wonder it's hard to figure out how to handle sticky situations! If you find yourself feeling overwhelmed or struggling with the social scene, be sure to talk to a trusted adult. (School counselors are boot camp experts!)

Conflict and Aggressive Behaviors Shared by Middle Schoolers:

"Last year, a really popular kid picked on and threatened me. He would judge me, but no one would stand up because they would get picked on too. Eventually, I asked my friends if they noticed he was picking on me, and they said yes, but they didn't want anything to do with it."

"It typically happens outside of school or in areas where teachers aren't around."

"The most hurtful things are said on social media. People also post pictures that others don't want to be shared."

"Girls look you up and down and give this sly smirk that says you're not cool enough."

"I feel like when this sort of stuff happens, it's not straight to the person's face. It's more talking behind their back, avoiding them, and exclusion."

Conflict Under the Microscope: What's Really Going On

Having fun yet? This is tough stuff! Button up your lab coats. Let's dig deeper into this scene.

You are likely to encounter conflict and drama since you do not attend United Unicorns Middle School. Disagreements, misunderstandings, mistakes, and mean behaviors are unavoidable in life and are a chance to learn and grow from the experience. (Especially in middle school, where there are so many humans going through puberty under one roof!) If you find yourself in a conflict, it helps to think about these questions:

1. What happened? (Be specific.)

2. Who was affected or harmed by what happened?

3. What was your part? What can you take responsibility for?

4. What is one thing you can do to help make things right? How can you learn from this?

Bullying, however, is a different story. Bullying behavior **needs to be stopped**, and adult assistance is likely necessary. With the growth of technology, bullying has expanded online. Ugh! Cyberbullying uses technology—such as social media, text messages, email, or websites—to humiliate, threaten, or degrade another person. Cyberbullying is especially harmful because it can occur anonymously and go viral at the touch of a key.

Random (Not Really) Facts about Unicorns:

This is tough stuff! To lighten things up for a moment, let's talk about unicorns. According to random websites, unicorns have sky blue or purple eyes. A baby unicorn is called a sparkle. (Seriously!) And last but not least, according to mythology, whoever touches a unicorn will find happiness throughout life. Okay, enough of that. Let's get back to reality.

Why Do Kids Bully?

According to many experts, including Signe Whitson, people bully others to *gain social status*, to *have power over another*, and to *get attention*. (Boy, these themes keep popping up in this book!)

Why Do Kids Bully?
• Social status
• Power and control
• Attention

But at a deeper level, *what makes some kids behave this way? What drives someone to be intentionally aggressive to another person repeatedly?* Chances are it's because of one of the reasons below:

Deeper Reasons for Bullying
• They treat others how they've been treated. Someone's bullied them.
• They are struggling or have low self-esteem.
• They don't understand how to socialize or how to behave in appropriate ways.

It hurts when kids are behaving aggressively, but it helps to understand why. It likely has nothing to do with you. (That's REALLY important to remember in middle school!)

A Hidden Form of Bullying:

One form of bullying is so hidden, it is often overlooked. Do you ever repeatedly say bad things about yourself inside your head? Things like, "I'm so stupid, I'm ugly, I hate myself." This is self-bullying and also harms self-esteem and well-being. It's essential to be aware of when these thoughts cloud your thinking and, instead, try to treat yourself with the same respect that you treat others. And if these thoughts persist, get help from a trusted adult.

You Choose the Ending: Cyber War

Some kids thought it would be funny to create a social media page called "The 8th Grade Burn Book." Embarrassing photos and rude comments about kids are posted on the page. Over time, the page targets just one girl. This quickly goes viral.

You feel helpless as you watch this unfold online. The girl finds out about the page and misses a few days of school. Things settle down a bit, but then it ramps back up when she returns.

You choose the ending: What do you do?

ENDING A:

You send a direct message to the kids that created the page and tell them to take it down. (Turn to page 106.)

ENDING B:

You talk to a teacher that you know will listen. (Turn to page 106.)

ENDING C:

You don't do anything and hope the situation gets better. (Turn to page 107.)

ENDING D (OPTIONAL):

(Don't like these endings? Add a new ending, then turn to page 107.)

_____

_____

_____

_____

_____

Antidotes from Middle Schoolers: How to Deal with Conflict and Aggressive Behaviors

Conflict and aggressive behaviors are often painful and challenging to navigate. Middle schoolers shared the following antidotes. **Place a check mark** by the approaches that will best help you if you are the target of or witness aggressive behavior. Feel free to add another antidote.

☐ "Don't let others get to you, and always have a comeback at the ready. Keep your head up high."

☐ "Stick with trustworthy friends that will stand up for you and support you. Speak to an adult if you need help."

☐ "As my mom always says, you don't have to be friends with everybody, but there is no reason to be mean."

☐ "If you don't know how to make it stop, report it. And if you see someone else being bullied, report that too."

☐ _____

_____

_____

_____

 You Choose the Ending: Cyber War (Cont.)

This quickly goes viral. You feel helpless as you watch this unfold online. The girl finds out about the page and misses a few days of school. Things settle down a bit, but then it ramps back up when she returns.

You choose the ending: What do you do?

ENDING A:

You send a direct message to the kids that created the page and tell them to take it down. You type, *NOT funny and NOT cool. Time to take this down.* One kid replies, *W/E. Heard of free speech?*

School officials find out about the page and immediately contact the families of the students involved. The page is deleted. The next day, all of the teachers make a point to talk about cyberbullying in class. The kids who started the page are assigned consequences according to the school's zero tolerance policy. The school even brings in some speakers to talk about bullying.

ENDING B:

You talk to a teacher that you know will listen. You ask the teacher to keep your report confidential because you're afraid the perpetrators will come after you. The teacher alerts school officials who immediately contact the families of the students who started the page. They are assigned consequences according to the school's zero tolerance policy. The next day, when you see the girl, you ask her how she's doing and let her know you feel bad that she was the target of this.

ENDING C:

You don't do anything and hope the situation gets better. After a few days, the page is old news, and you think that's the end of it. But it's not. You notice that when the girl walks down the hall, she's mocked by others who say rude things under their breath and laugh. She starts to miss school a lot, and when she's there, she looks depressed. You begin to think about what you can do to help.

ENDING D (OPTIONAL):

_____

_____

_____

_____

_____

Important Stuff to Remember about Conflict:

1. Middle schoolers tend to treat other students in positive or neutral ways, but there's no shortage of unsavory behaviors.

2. The behaviors explored in this book, *and simply being human,* contribute to conflicts, misunderstandings, and mistakes. These situations can be painful but sometimes lead to positive changes. (Having a trusted adult to talk with can help navigate this rocky road!)

3. Bullying spikes in middle school, but that doesn't make it okay. If you are bullied or see someone else being bullied, seek support. (Luckily, these behaviors happen less as you move through high school. . . . Phew!)

The Final Word

Whether you have been the target of aggressive behavior or the aggressor, this event *does not* define you. Every day brings a new opportunity to start again.

Challenge for Change:

Challenge 1: This book talks a lot about "trusted adults." A trusted adult is someone you feel comfortable talking to about your feelings and struggles. You trust that this person will listen and help as you navigate tough situations. If you find yourself in a difficult situation, who would you talk to?

Challenge 2: How is bullying handled in your school? Do students feel safe enough to report bullying and know that it will be handled well, or do students avoid reporting it? What would improve the environment in your school?

Chapter 9:

Weird Behavior #9– Peer Pressure Party

· ·

Let's get back to our research on another warm and fuzzy topic. Not surprisingly, peer pressure is as common as growth spurts and gossip in middle school. (Okay, maybe not quite as common as gossip.) Let's start with your experience on this tricky subject.

 (This Is Not a Test) Research Questions:

	YES	NO
A friend tells a joke, and everyone laughs. You don't understand the joke. Do you laugh anyway because you don't want the group to know you don't get it?	☐	☐
Has a friend or peer ever tried to pressure you into doing something you didn't want to do?	☐	☐

YES   NO

Have you ever pressured someone into doing something they didn't want to do? ☐ ☐

If you answered YES to any of these questions, you've experienced the effects of peer pressure. Peer pressure can be positive, like when your friend encourages you to study for a test. It can also be negative, like when your friend urges you to skip class. Let's take a closer look.

Peer Pressure Under the Microscope: What's Really Going On

Peer pressure feeds on the things that scare us, like being excluded or rejected. Humans are social creatures; we want to fit in, have friends, and gain approval from others. Combine all of these fears under one roof and ta-da! The ideal environment for peer pressure to thrive is born.

Definition of peer pressure:

When someone feels they need to do the same things as people their age or in their social group to be liked or accepted.

"Peer pressure doesn't come into your life like a bomb. It's subtle and hard to spot. You may not even know you are in it. It can cause a little discomfort or a life-changing mistake. Most peer pressure is FOMO (fear of missing out). People do things just to stay in the group." (8th grader)

Clarification:

Peer pressure tends to increase over the course of middle school. It may not be much of a factor in 6th grade but a big deal in 8th grade.

Examples of Peer Pressure Shared by Middle Schoolers:

"Friendship has a big impact on peer pressure. A lot of people are pressured to hang out with certain people and then need to do certain things to become part of that group."

"I'm in 8th grade, and some of my friends are starting to experiment with drugs and alcohol. There is a ton of peer pressure to do things I don't necessarily want to do."

"Peer pressure in middle school comes from wanting to fit in and feel like you have a big group of friends. I have noticed that if my friend does not like another person, they will talk bad about them, and I feel pressured to agree with them."

"Personally, I don't know a whole lot about it. I have a small group of friends, and we are not the 'popular kids.' The popular kids do it the most."

In a nutshell, middle schoolers think kids conform to peer pressure to *stay part of a group* and *fit in*. Combine this with new, sometimes risky behaviors, and pressure ramps up even more. Exhibit P lists the most common forms of peer pressure in middle school. It's important to mention that most students are not participating in these behaviors. The abundance of gossip makes it seem like more students are participating when it's typically a minority of students.

Exhibit P: Common Focus of Peer Pressure in Middle School
Vaping/smoking, drugs & alcohol
Dating
Sexting   *(e.g., sharing nude photos online)*
Acting disinterested in school   *(e.g., hiding academic skills to be cool, acting like school and grades don't matter)*
Aggressive behavior   *(e.g., contributing to behavior or remaining silent when others are bullied)*
Dangerous behavior   *(e.g., activities that could be harmful to self or others or illegal)*

Scientific Facts about Pressure:

Peer pressure is just one form of pressure. There's also air and liquid pressure. The scientific unit to measure internal pressure is called the pascal, named after French physicist and mathematician Blaise Pascal. A pascal is a unit of pressure equivalent to one newton per square meter. If pascals could be used to measure peer pressure, how many units would be in your middle school? (Pascal's perfect peer pressure party! Say that three times fast.)

Hmmm . . . have you noticed that *fitting in* and *being accepted* are the underlying reasons for many of the behaviors dissected in this book?! Humans give in to peer pressure for these same reasons. But yielding to negative peer pressure to gain acceptance can backfire because of two hypotheses.

Hypothesis #1: Giving in to peer pressure means a person will fit in and feel better about themselves.

Finding #1: Giving in to peer pressure may leave people with the feeling that they've betrayed themselves to conform to what others want.

Hypothesis #2: Those who don't give in to peer pressure will lose their friends and become outcasts.

Finding #2: People often come to admire or have more respect for someone who stands up for what they believe in or holds their ground. They may not say it right away, but people may slowly start to copy this behavior.

Random (Not Really) Facts about Unicorns:

Let's lighten things up for a moment with a few more unicorn "facts." If a unicorn and a pegasus mate, the baby becomes a flying unicorn. (Cool!) According to various websites, unicorns live in groups of four or five. Unicorn families spend their lives living peacefully in the forest. (They must not have middle school there!) Okay, back to real life.

You Choose the Ending: The Big Jump

One summer day, you meet up with a group of kids at the river. Sometimes, the river is deep enough for people to jump from the bridge above without getting hurt. It's rained recently, so the water seems to be flowing higher than usual.

The city prohibits people from jumping, but some kids do it anyway. You've never done it because it just seems like a bad idea. Before long, one kid dares another to jump. This kid is always doing crazy stuff, and it's not surprising that they jump.

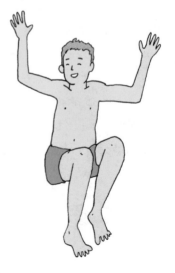

All of a sudden, all eyes are on you. The group chants your name and urges you to jump. You don't want to, but you're not sure what to do. The group doesn't let up, and soon, they are calling you a chicken.

You choose the ending: What do you do?

ENDING A:

You say no thanks and that you are not into jumping off bridges. (Turn to page 119.)

ENDING B:

You secretly text your mom the code for when you feel backed into a corner. (Turn to page 119.)

ENDING C:

You jump. (Turn to page 120.)

ENDING D (OPTIONAL):

(Don't like these endings? Add a new ending, then turn to page 120.)

_____

_____

_____

_____

_____

_____

_____

_____

Antidotes from Middle Schoolers: How to Deal with Peer Pressure

Being pressured to do something that you don't want to do feels pretty awful. Middle schoolers shared the following antidotes. **Place a check mark** by the approaches that would best help you deal when you feel pressured. Feel free to add another antidote too.

☐ "Don't ignore it when you feel uncomfortable. Your gut is trying to tell you something. Listen!"

☐ "Most of the peer pressure that happens later in middle school is about drugs and alcohol. It takes a toll on your reputation and trust. Just try to stay out of it, and THINK before you ACT, always!"

☐ "Don't feel obligated to be friends with everyone. Everyone is NOT doing it (drugs, vaping, etc.). Have a voice, and don't have toxic friends."

☐ _____

_____

_____

_____

_____

_____

_____

You Choose the Ending: The Big Jump (Cont.)

All of a sudden, all eyes are on you. The group chants your name and urges you to jump. You don't want to, but you're not sure what to do. The group doesn't let up, and soon, they are calling you a chicken.

You choose the ending: What do you do?

ENDING A:

You say no thanks and that you are not into jumping off bridges. You joke that you like your brains intact as you head down the stairs to the water. Several people call you a wimp but then quickly start pressuring another person to jump. That kid follows your lead and heads down the stairs. Soon, the group moves on and begins swimming.

ENDING B:

You secretly text your mom the code for when you feel backed into a corner. When the group is distracted, you type *!!* into your phone. On cue, your

mom calls and asks you to come home. You tell your friends you have to go and feel a big sense of relief. You and your mom created this plan in case you ever ended up in a situation that felt unsafe. This was the perfect moment to test it out.

ENDING C:

You jump. You're terrified, but you don't want to be seen as a chicken. Your body slaps the water, and your feet scrape the bottom. You feel a rush of adrenaline and a massive sense of relief as you rise to the surface. The group starts to pressure another kid. This kid says no and something funny. The group moves on and starts swimming. As you dry off, you feel queasy. You can't believe that you allowed the group to talk you into doing something that you didn't want to do. It didn't really matter in the end.

ENDING D (OPTIONAL):

_____

_____

_____

_____

_____

Important Stuff to Remember about Peer Pressure:

1. Peer pressure can be positive or negative (for example, being pressured to study versus being pressured to cheat).

2. Peer pressure ramps up in middle school as kids try to fit in and be accepted (Pascal's perfect peer pressure party!).

3. Having friends that make wise choices and that respect your choices is an important part of this science equation (and it will reduce the amount of pressure on you!).

The Final Word:

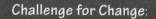

When the dust settles, kids respect the kids who dare to say no to things they don't want to do.

Challenge for Change:

Challenge 1: Peer pressure is common in middle school. Think about what you might do or say if you get into an uncomfortable situation filled with peer pressure.

Challenge 2: If you notice your friends pressuring someone to do something they don't want to do this week, ask them to stop.

Chapter 10:

Weird Behaviors (1+2+3+4+5+6+7+8+9) + Tests + Grades = STRESS!

• •

Welcome to "Rate Your Stress Level"! Read the scenarios below and **place a check mark** by the response that honestly describes how you would feel in each situation.

Rate Your Stress Level Scenarios:

1. Your good friend suddenly starts avoiding you.

NO WORRIES	SORT OF STRESSED	PRETTY STRESSED	REALLY STRESSED
☐	☐	☐	☐

2. It's almost the end of the term, and your grades are far below where you want them to be.

NO WORRIES	SORT OF STRESSED	PRETTY STRESSED	REALLY STRESSED
☐	☐	☐	☐

3. Your schedule is so packed with activities. You hardly have time to do your homework, let alone relax.

NO WORRIES   SORT OF STRESSED   PRETTY STRESSED   REALLY STRESSED

☐   ☐   ☐   ☐

If you checked any response other than "No Worries," congratulations! You are a human being. Like it or not, feeling stress is sometimes part of life. Schoolwork, social stuff, family stuff, and even being busy with fun activities can feel stressful. And in middle school, sometimes all of these scenarios happen at the same time! Super stress!

Stress Under the Microscope: What's Really Going On

Definition of stress:

(Noun) A state of mental or emotional strain resulting from difficult or demanding circumstances.

Sometimes, stress can be useful and inspire us to tackle challenges. For example, if you feel stressed about your grades, you might put more effort into school to improve them. Or if you have an audition coming up, you might practice more, improving your confidence. But stress can also feel overwhelming, making you constantly worry about how things will turn out.

Scientific Facts about Stress:

Stress is your body's response to challenges or threats. Sometimes, this response is small, and sometimes, it is huge. When you sense a big threat, whether real or imagined, the body kicks into high gear. This response is known as the "fight or flight" reaction or the "stress response." Your nervous system releases stress hormones, your heart beats faster, your muscles tighten, your breath quickens, and your senses become sharper. (Geez, even reading about stress feels stressful!)

Examples of Stress
Shared by Middle Schoolers:

"It's tough if you miss a day of school. There's lots of work to make up. It wasn't like this in elementary school."

"After-school activities add to my stress. I feel really time-crunched. Social stuff is stressful too."

"Grades matter now. I'm constantly worried about missing assignments and am always checking my grades online."

"My parents are getting a divorce. I can't stop thinking about it, so I'm not paying much attention in class."

In a nutshell, middle schoolers report that *schoolwork, social stuff, activities,* and *family life* cause stress. Often, stress feels manageable, but sometimes, it feels overwhelming. When stress feels overwhelming, it's important to find support and to take care of yourself while getting your stress level back to a manageable level.

Scientifically Proven Trick to Calm Down:

Did you know that simply taking a few deep breaths can impact how you feel? Taking deep breaths lowers your heart rate and blood pressure and even reduces cortisol, your body's stress hormone. Who knew that something so easy could have such an effect! So, when you find yourself feeling stressed . . . remember, DEEP BREATHS!

You Choose the Ending: Not a Good Day

You overslept this morning, which made you late for school. Because you got to class late, you didn't have time to finish the math test in first period, earning a lousy grade. At lunch, your friends are acting strange. You wonder if you did something that upset them. And after school, you have tryouts for your

favorite sport. If you don't do well, you won't make the team. This has not been a good day so far. You feel frazzled and nervous about tryouts.

You choose the ending: What do you do?

ENDING A:

You talk with your math teacher. (Turn to page 130.)

ENDING B:

You try to relax before tryouts. (Turn to page 130.)

ENDING C:

You get to tryouts early so you have extra time to warm up. (Turn to page 131.)

ENDING D (OPTIONAL):

(Don't like these endings? Add a new ending, then turn to page 131.)

_____

_____

_____

_____

_____

Antidotes from Middle Schoolers: How to Deal with Stress

Some stress is normal, but too much makes life feel overwhelming. Middle schoolers shared the following antidotes. **Place a check mark** by the approaches that would best help you deal with stress. Feel free to add another antidote too.

☐ "Try to have a system to keep up with all assignments and check for missing work if you miss a day of school. Always know that things aren't really that bad. Just the feeling of missing something can blow problems out of proportion."

☐ "Do not get caught up in social drama. Find good friends with similar qualities. Also, make sure you have hobbies to take your mind off stress and school."

☐ "If stress is getting to be too much, talk to the school counselor or someone you trust."

☐ _____

_____

_____

_____

_____

Exhibit S: Scientifically Proven Ways to Reduce Stress

(Seriously, this stuff helps!)

1. Take several slow, deep breaths

2. Exercise

3. Get enough sleep

4. Talk to someone about your feelings (when you name your feelings, it helps to tame them)

5. Take a break and do something you enjoy (listen to music, draw, spend time with a pet)

6. Learn to feel good about doing a "good job" instead of trying to do things perfectly (perfection is impossible!)

7. Break large tasks into smaller, manageable steps

Important Fact about Adolescents and Stress:

Did you know that anxiety is one of the top mental health concerns for adolescents? Many teens struggle with stress and get help to manage their stress levels. If you often feel overwhelmed by anxiety, be sure to get help from the school counselor or another trusted adult!

You Choose the Ending: Not a Good Day (Cont.)

If you don't do well, you won't make the team. This has not been a good day so far. You feel frazzled and nervous about tryouts.

You choose the ending: What do you do?

ENDING A:

You talk with your math teacher. You apologize for being late this morning and share your worries about your test grade. Your teacher agrees to let you finish your math test before school tomorrow. Your mind stops racing, and you start to feel more settled. You begin to focus on getting ready for tryouts. You want to make the team but realize that all you can do is your best. So, with a deep breath, that's what you intend to do.

ENDING B:

You try to relax before tryouts. After school, you chill out in your room and listen to your favorite song. The lyrics are perfect for this stressful day. You notice your body starts to relax, and your head clears a little. Next, you play a song that will get you pumped up for tryouts. Before heading out, you double-check your alarm clock to make sure it will go off in the morning, and you make a plan to check in with your math teacher before class.

ENDING C:

You get to tryouts early so you have extra time to warm up. Your body is wound so tight; you feel like you might explode. Running feels great and starts to release some of the negative energy. You think about how your friends were acting at lunch and decide not to jump to any conclusions. Maybe tomorrow  will be better. You take some deep breaths and begin to feel like yourself again.

ENDING D (OPTIONAL):

_____

_____

_____

_____

_____

_____

_____

Important Stuff to Remember about Stress:

1. Stress is the body's natural response to demands and threats. (It evolved to help early humans survive harsh conditions. Today, it helps people survive middle school!)

2. Stress can be useful and inspire us to tackle challenges. Or it can leave us feeling worried and stuck. (If you can find a way to laugh, humor is a proven stress reliever!)

3. When feeling stressed, it helps to recognize the feeling and find ways to relieve it. Talking with a friend, taking deep breaths, and exercising are ways to relieve stress.

The Final Word

Feeling stress is normal from time to time. Notice these feelings and find ways to take care of yourself when they come up. If stress becomes overwhelming, be sure to seek support from a trusted adult.

Challenge for Change:

Challenge 1: Think about your life. What area of your life feels the most stressful (schoolwork/grades, home/

family, activities/sports, social stuff/friends, etc.)? What do you do to take care of yourself when you are feeling stressed?

Challenge 2: Are there any changes you could make to your life that would reduce the amount of stress you feel? What would you change?

Chapter 11:

But Hey, There's Cool Stuff Too

· ·

As you've noticed by now, this book explores the tricky side of middle school. Luckily, there's really cool stuff too! Let's shift our focus to the positive side. What do you like best about middle school? Here's what some middle schoolers said.

What do you like best about middle school?

"Lunch!"

"My favorite part is making new friends, having a good laugh at lunch, and most of all, dances. So much fun!"

"I love that we have classes like art, shop, and health."

"Pep rallies, teachers, and gym class."

"Freedom! No more standing in lines like in elementary school, and teachers put more trust in you."

"I like how you can be more independent."

"Some of my teachers are really cool and supportive. They make coming to class fun."

"Middle school is a good time to find friends that you enjoy being with and who bring out the best in you. When I started middle school, I decided to switch friend groups because I never really fit in with my old group. I landed in a group I love to be with."

Top Ten Cool Things about Middle School
#10: No standing or walking in lines!
#9: Diverse classes and teachers
#8: Lockers
#7: Dances
#6: The chance to be who you want to be
#5: School clubs
#4: School sports
#3: More responsibility
#2: More independence
#1: New friends

Think about your own middle school experience. What do you like best? List your favorite things below.

YOUR Top Ten Cool Things about Middle School
#10:
#9:
#8:
#7:
#6:
#5:
#4:
#3:
#2:
#1:

Scientific Fact about Optimism:

Optimism is the tendency to look on the bright side of things. Researchers who study optimistic people have found that there are health benefits to positive thinking. Optimists experience less stress, have fewer illnesses, and even live longer! Because optimists don't give up as quickly as pessimists, they tend to achieve more success too. Now there's something to smile about!

Do you remember how you felt when you started middle school? Nervous? Excited? Scared? All of the above?! But then you settled in, and elementary school became a distant memory. Middle school life became the new normal. (Maybe even all of the odd behaviors became normal!) The following thoughts were shared by students regarding what they wish they'd known when they started middle school. Add your thoughts too.

What I wish I'd known when I started middle school:

"I wish I'd been more open-minded, like being more open to new people, new activities, and all the other changes that come with a new school."

"I would tell someone not to stress out, because when I started, I was always nervous and worried. But now, when I look back, there was no reason to stress because everything worked out."

"I think the most important thing is to know that people change and that change is okay."

"Pay attention in class. It will make your life a lot easier."

"Don't ever give out your locker combination or your phone passcode!"

"It's okay for friendships to change. It's okay to like somebody, and it's okay to be yourself. Don't be afraid to speak your mind."

"It's good to have friends that have your back, but make sure YOU have your back too."

_____

_____

_____

_____

_____

Middle school is a time of change. (Now that's an understatement!) As you navigate these changes, like more responsibility, more independence, and more choices, you'll learn new things about yourself. Here are some things some students learned about themselves since starting middle school. Feel free to add to this list.

What I've learned about myself since starting middle school:

"I've learned how to be more organized to keep up with all of my classes."

"I'm getting better at navigating the whole social scene. I used to take things really personally, but now I'm learning to keep an open mind."

"I'm trying to just be myself and not be what others think I should be."

"I learned that I don't have to participate in the drama. Getting involved in the drama is a choice. Now, I choose not to get involved."

_____

_____

_____

A Few Random Jokes about Middle School:

1. Why did the broom get poor grades in middle school?

Answer: Because it was always sweeping in class!

2. Why shouldn't you write with a broken pencil?

Answer: Because it's pointless!

3. Which are the strongest days of the week?

Answer: Saturday and Sunday. The rest are weak days!

4. Where do you put smart hot dogs?

Answer: On honor rolls!

5. What makes Mr. Cyclops such an effective middle school teacher?

Answer: He only has one pupil!

Okay, that's enough bad jokes for one day. Before we wrap up this chapter, there's one more cool thing about middle school. It only lasts a few years! Like a roller coaster filled with twists and turns, climbs and drops, and a bit of nausea, middle school ends in a flash. Whether you love every second or want to get off as soon as possible, the ride is short. Buckle up, hold on tight, and hang in there. It will be over before you know it.

Chapter 12:

The Final Word— How to Deal and Define Yourself

• •

There you have it! This scientific exploration has officially confirmed that middle school is bursting with weird stuff. (Well, duh!) But when these behaviors are dissected, several common themes pop up over and over. Students are trying out ways to *fit in, be accepted, belong, gain status, get attention, etc.* Basically, they are being human. This doesn't make things any easier or less awkward, but it helps to understand what you and your fellow humans are seeking.

Middle school is sort of like a giant social experiment. Fill a large school with a diverse bunch of adolescents. Increase the volume of hormones and emotions. Introduce variables such as drama, popularity, crushes, and other new behaviors. Shake it all up, stand back, and observe. (Or duck!)

It's no surprise that strange stuff happens! But something cool eventually occurs too. Through all the craziness, you learn how *you* want to be. You learn how to navigate changing friendships. You learn how you want to handle social media, gossip, and peer pressure. You survive heartbreak and crushes. You begin to define *who you are*. (Good thing you didn't attend United Unicorns Middle School!)

Of course, mistakes and mess-ups are inevitable. Humans are imperfect, especially in middle school! Go easy on yourself and others. And when all else fails, connect with people and activities that make you smile. When things get really weird, sometimes finding ways to laugh is the best medicine. And be sure to seek support from a trusted adult when you feel overwhelmed. We ALL need help from time to time.

Scientific Facts about Laughter:

Did you know that laughter has positive effects on your mind and body? When you laugh, the level of stress hormones in your body decreases, which reduces feelings of anxiety. Your body also releases chemicals called endorphins, which make you feel good. And you activate T-cells that help you fight off sickness. Doctors aren't kidding when they say laughter is the best medicine!

The Final, Final Word

This book covered a lot! How can you possibly remember it all?! Don't worry—you don't have to. As you navigate your way through middle school, many of these strange behaviors may smack you in the face. (Hopefully not literally. . . . Ouch!)

Just re-read that chapter and figure out how you would like to proceed. All you can really control is yourself, but how you choose *to think and act* makes a difference in making middle school a better place. And be sure to forgive yourself when you goof up. This stuff is tricky, and everyone makes mistakes! Apologize as needed, and do better next time. The biggest lessons learned in life often grow out of mistakes.

The Final Words in Review

Weird Behavior #1—Harsh Judgment

We ALL have judgmental thoughts sometimes. And we ALL have the power to keep these thoughts to ourselves. Simply put, limiting judgmental conversations will make middle school a better place.

Weird Behavior #2—Changing Friendships

Everyone looks for different things in friendship, but deep down, everyone is trying to find the same stuff: *acceptance and belonging.* Friendships change a lot in middle school. Try not to take it personally, and stay open to new friendships.

Weird Behavior #3—
The Whole "Popularity" Thing

In middle school, there's a difference between "popularity" and being well-liked. The qualities of well-liked students gain the respect of their peers.

Weird Behavior #4—
Crushes & Warp-Speed Dating

Everyone's on their own timeline when it comes to crushes. If you decide to enter the world of crushes, find friends that you trust so you can share your feelings and know those feelings will be respected.

Weird Behavior #5—
The Ins and Outs of Cliques & Groups

It's natural to have a group of friends you prefer, but be sure to treat others well too. Treating others with dignity is possible, even in middle school.

Weird Behavior #6—
Gossip & Drama-O-Rama

When you are about to begin gossiping, STOP. Instead, find the courage to speak directly to the person you have a conflict with or remain silent. Talk about others the way you would want them to talk about you.

Weird Behavior #7—
Social Media, Phubbing, & FOMO

Social media serves some, but not all, social needs. Use social media to spread goodwill, and balance screen time with plenty of time offline doing things you enjoy.

Weird Behavior #8—
Conflict and Aggressive Behaviors . . . Ouch!

Whether you have been the target of aggressive behavior or the aggressor, this event *does not* define you. Every day brings a new opportunity to start again.

Weird Behavior #9—Peer Pressure Party

When the dust settles, kids respect the kids who dare to say no to things they don't want to do.

Weird Behavior #10—STRESS!

Feeling stress is normal from time to time. Notice these feelings and find ways to take care of yourself when they come up. If stress feels overwhelming, be sure to seek support from a trusted adult.

Afterword:

Ideas and Resources to Help Schools Combat Weird Behaviors

• •

Middle school and baffling behaviors go together like cats and hairballs. (Oops, sorry about that visual!) There are, however, things schools, teachers, and students can do to address the topics covered in this book. Some of these ideas are simple, and some take more effort, but all can improve the middle school social scene.

If you think some of these ideas would help your school, take action! Set up a meeting with your teacher or the school principal and make your case. Be sure to organize your thoughts before the meeting so you are ready. Feel free to add more ideas to the list too.

1. **Ever-Changing Lunchroom Table Configuration to Combat Territory Wars:** If groups behave like

they "own" certain tables at lunch, mix things up. After every lunchroom floor cleaning, have the janitor rearrange the tables in a new pattern. One day, arrange in rows. Another day, try a different pattern. It's hard to claim a territory when the terrain keeps changing!

2. **Inspiring Guest Speaker Series:** Powerful presenters have shown a positive short-term effect on student behavior. A series of speakers scheduled over the school year can help to prolong positive effects. Ideally, schedule experienced speakers that know how to connect with middle schoolers on issues that matter to them. Topics may include kindness, acceptance, diversity, peer pressure, and more.

3. **Non-Judgment Day:** As described in Chapter 1, the human mind is wired to make judgments about people and things. Sometimes these judgments are harsh and critical. With some attention and effort, these thoughts can be stopped inside our heads and never put into words. To bring awareness to the effects of harsh judgment, schools can schedule a "Non-Judgment Day." Before the official day, students and teachers can explore judgment and its impact. Create posters and reminders to raise awareness. Then, on the designated "Non-Judgment

Day," students and teachers pay close attention to their thoughts and try not to express harsh judgment in their words. At the end of the day, classes discuss the experience and lessons learned.

4. **Lunch Spaces:** Let's face it, not everyone loves eating in a packed, noisy lunchroom. Sometimes people need quiet or space. Schools are required to keep track of students during lunch and to provide supervision. Still, it may be possible to add a few alternative eating areas. Possibly, there is a quiet space outside the lunchroom with just a few tables and a different location for students to read or play games.

5. **Classroom Improvement Meetings:** Introduce an improvement box in the classroom and encourage students to write down ideas about changes they feel could improve relationships, academic success, and the classroom vibe. Every month, the teacher selects an idea from the box. The class discusses the suggestion and creates a plan of action.

6. **Safe-to-Tell Resource:** Schools need to have a safe and anonymous way for students to report concerns like bullying and threats of violence. A safe-to-tell resource or hotline ensures that concerns are heard and responded to appropriately.

School staff should regularly remind students about this resource so they remember it when they need it.

7. **Get to Know the School Counselor:** Most schools have a counselor on staff. School counselors are a valuable resource to address individual struggles as well as broader challenges. Counselors also have access to a lot of helpful resources. Be sure to connect with your school counselor about ideas to improve your middle school experience, and check in from time to time so they get to know you personally too.

Discussion Questions

. . . .

Important: *When responding to these questions, be sure not to share names to protect the privacy of others (and to avoid drama-o-rama).*

Chapter 1: Weird Behavior #1— Harsh Judgement

1. On a scale of 1 to 5, how much harsh judgment is floating around the halls of your middle school? (1 = not that much; 5 = tons) Explain why you chose that number.

2. What type of stuff do students tend to judge others about? How much judgment is actually "jumping to conclusions," or people assuming others judge them when they are not.

Chapter 2: Weird Behavior #2—Changing Friendships

1. Have you experienced friendship changes in the last year? What was the hardest part of that change? Did anything positive come out of it?

Chapter 3: Weird Behavior #3—The Whole "Popularity" Thing

1. This chapter describes two different types of popularity, well-liked students and high-status students. Does this description fit the popularity scene at your school? If not, describe the scene.

2. If you could change something about popularity at your school, what would you change?

Chapter 4: Weird Behavior #4—Crushes & Warp Speed Dating

1. This chapter explores that there is pressure in some groups to start dating. Does that happen at your school? Why do you think there is pressure to date in middle school?

Chapter 5: Weird Behavior #5—
The Ins and Outs of Cliques & Groups

1. What is the group scene like at your school? Do groups have different labels and ranks? What are the negative effects of this group scene? Are there positive effects?

Chapter 6: Weird Behavior #6—
Gossip & Drama-O-Rama

1. Everyone gossips from time to time. Gossip that is judgmental, one-sided, and shared behind someone's back is especially toxic. On a scale of 1 to 5, how much gossip is shared at your school? (1 = not much; 5 = tons)

2. How do you handle gossip about others? How do you deal with gossip about you?

Chapter 7: Weird Behavior #7—
Social Media, Phubbing, & FOMO

1. Social media has both positive and negative effects. What positive impact does social media have in your middle school? What are the negative impacts?

2. When your parents were in middle school, social media didn't exist. Do you think middle school back then was better, the same, or worse?

Chapter 8: Weird Behavior #8— Conflict and Aggressive Behaviors...Ouch!

1. This chapter breaks down the difference between rude, mean, and bullying behavior. What advice would you share with a new student about how to deal with these behaviors?

2. Is there something your school could do to improve the environment?

Chapter 9: Weird Behavior #9— Peer Pressure Party

1. What things are kids pressured to do at your school?

2. Have you felt pressure from your friends or peers to do things you didn't want to do?

3. Are kids that stand up to peer pressure respected? Explain.

Chapter 10: Weird Behavior #10—STRESS!

1. Rate your stress level on a scale of 1 to 5. (1 = not much; 5 = tons). If you feel a lot of stress,

where does it come from? (pressure I put on myself, pressure from my family, pressure from peers, something else, all of the above)

2. Do you have things that you do to manage your stress? Explain.

Afterword—Ideas and Resources to Help Schools Combat Weird Behaviors

1. The book's afterward shares ideas to improve middle school campuses. Which of these ideas do you think would improve your middle school? Feel free to share a new idea.

References

"5 Things You Should Know about Stress." National Institute of Mental Health. 2019. www.nimh.nih.gov /health/publications/stress/index.shtml.

Anderson, Monica, and Jingjing Jiang. "Teens, Social Media & Technology 2018." Pew Research Center: Internet, Science & Tech. Accessed August 14, 2020. www.pewresearch.org/internet/2018/05/31/teens -social-media-technology-2018/.

Apter, Terri. "Disrupting the Feed—Teenage Girls' Use of Social Media: An Intervention to Improve Social Media Health." The Female Lead. 2019. https://www. thefemaleleadsociety.com/wp-content /uploads/2019/10/Research-Results-July-2019.pdf.

Apter, Terri. "How to Reduce the Toxicity of Teen Girls' Social Media Use." Psychology Today. October 20, 2019. www.psychologytoday.com/us/blog/domestic -intelligence/201910/how-reduce-the-toxicity-teen -girls-social-media-use.

Bergland, Christopher. "Optimism Study Gives Optimists More Reason to Be Optimistic." *Psychology Today.* August 27, 2019. www.psychologytoday.com/us/blog /the-athletes-way/201908/optimism-study-gives -optimists-more-reason-be-optimistic.

"Children and Teens." Anxiety and Depression Association of America. 2015. adaa.org/find-help/by -demographics/children/children-teens.

"The Common Sense Census: Media Use by Tweens and Teens, 2019." Common Sense Media. Accessed October 28, 2019. www.commonsensemedia.org /research/the-common-sense-census-media-use-by -tweens-and-teens-2019.

Dawes, Molly, and Hongling Xie. 2016. "The Trajectory of Popularity Goal During the Transition to Middle School." *The Journal of Early Adolescence* 37, no. 6: 852–83. https:// doi.org/10.1177/0272431615626301.

"Dealing with Peer Pressure in School." AccreditedSchoolsOnline.org. Updated November 24, 2020. www.accreditedschoolsonline.org/resources /peer-pressure/.

Denworth, Lydia. "The Outsize Influence of Your Middle-School Friends." *The Atlantic.* January 28, 2020. www. theatlantic.com/family/archive/2020/01/friendship

-crucial-adolescent-brain/605638/.

Hasan, Shirin, ed. "Anxiety Disorders Factsheet (for Schools)." KidsHealth from Nemours. Reviewed May 2019. kidshealth.org/en/parents/anxiety-factsheet.html.

Kamenetz, Anya. "It's a Smartphone Life: More Than Half of U.S. Children Now Have One." NPR. October 31, 2019. www.npr.org/2019/10/31/774838891/its-a-smartphone-life-more-than-half-of-u-s-children-now-have-one?utmsource=nprnewsletter.

Kennedy-Moore, Eileen. "Popular Kids: Why Are Some Children Popular?" *Psychology Today*. December 1, 2013. www.psychologytoday.com/us/blog/growing-friendships/201312/popular-kids.

Kuhn, Charlie. "What's the Difference between Dignity and Respect?" Cultures of Dignity. September 4, 2019. culturesofdignity.com/difference-between-dignity-and-respect/.

LaFontana, Kathryn, and Antonius Cillessen. 2002. "Children's Perceptions of Popular and Unpopular Peers: A Multimethod Assessment." *Developmental Psychology* 38, no. 5: 635–47. https://doi.org/10.1037/0012-1649.38.5.635.

Lee, Lewina O., Peter James, Emily S. Zevon, Eric S. Kim, Claudia Trudel-Fitzgerald, Avron Spiro III, Francine Grodstein, and Laura D. Kubzansky. 2019. "Optimism Is Associated with Exceptional Longevity in 2

Epidemiologic Cohorts of Men and Women." *PNAS* 116, no. 37: 18357–62. https://doi.org/10.1073/pnas.1900712116.

Leor, Kevin. 2015. "Guest Speakers: A Great Way to Commit to Education." *Journal on Best Teaching Practices* 2, no. 2: 21–3. teachingonpurpose.org/wp-content/uploads/2015/06/Leor-K.-2015.-Guest-Speakers-A-Great-Way-to-Commit-to-Education.pdf.

Lyness, D'Arcy, ed. "Dealing with Peer Pressure." KidsHealth from Nemours. July 2015. kidshealth.org/en/kids/peer-pressure.html.

Patchin, Justin. "School Bullying Rates Increase by 35% from 2016 to 2019." Cyberbullying Research Center. 2019. https://cyberbullying.org/school-bullying-rates-increase-by-35-from-2016-to-2019.

Prinstein, Mitch. *Popular: The Power of Likability in a Status-Obsessed World*. New York: Viking, 2017.

Seldin, Melissa, and Christina Yanez. "Student Reports of Bullying: Results from the 2017 School Crime Supplement to the National Crime Victimization Survey." National Center for Education Statistics. July 2019. nces.ed.gov/pubsearch/pubsinfo.asp?pubid=2019054.

StopBullying.gov. "What Is Bullying." US Department of Health and Human Services. Accessed September 15, 2020. www.stopbullying.gov/bullying/what-is-bullying.

Whitson, Signe. *8 Keys to End Bullying: Strategies for Parents & Schools*. New York: W.W. Norton & Company, 2014.

"Why Do Kids Bully?" Stomp Out Bullying. 2019. www. stompoutbullying.org/why-kids-bully.

Wiseman, Rosalind. "Webinar: Developing Students' Social and Emotional Skills through the Owning Up Curriculum." Cultures of Dignity. October 28, 2020. culturesofdignity.com/webinar-owning-up-curriculum/.

Wolpert, Stuart. "'Cool' Kids in Middle School Bully More, Psychologists Report." ScienceDaily. January 24, 2013. www.sciencedaily.com /releases/2013/01/130124140729.htm.

Acknowledgments

· ·

Before I thank any one person, I would like to thank the universe for the following: Today's version of the bi-level haircut is much better than the one I sported in middle school. Pimples mostly subside after the teen years. And finally, the rough patches in life tend to shape and strengthen us in ways we never imagined.

This book lived inside of my head for years. Dislodging it from my brain would not have been possible without the following amazing people.

First, I am so grateful to the Familius team for seeing the need for this book and supporting my research and writing. Special thanks to Brooke Jorden, Shaelyn Topolovec, Lindsay Sandberg, Sarah Echard, Jaiden Wong, Adina Oberman, Ashley Mireles, and Christopher Robbins for your work bringing this book from concept to completion. The awesome illustrations by Lesley Imgart and beautiful book design and cover by Mara Harris are the icing on the cake.

Next, this book would be useless if not for the middle school students that shared their insights and experiences. I'm so grateful for the teachers that invited me into their classrooms, especially Ms. Maddox and Ms. Ruzicka.

My litmus test readers, including Dr. Cherylee Hirsch; Emily Schenk, MA, CRC; Sloane; Shea; Chris; Cade; and Sally, are rock stars. Each helped make sure the content was relevant and real. Thank you for reading, re-reading, answering my endless questions, and sharing your feedback.

And lastly, I'm so grateful for the researchers, writers, and practitioners who focus their work on adolescents. The body of knowledge about this important phase of life is deep and ever-evolving. These impressive people and the latest research inspired me to write a book about the nitty-gritty of middle school *for* middle schoolers.

About the Author

....

Jessica Speer is the award-winning author of *BFF or NRF (Not Really Friends)? A Girls Guide to Happy Friendships*. Her interactive books engage and entertain readers by combining the stories of preteens and teens with fun activities, like quizzes and fill-in-the blanks. Blending humor, a dash of science and practical insights, her writing unpacks the tricky stuff that peaks during adolescence.

She has a master's degree in social sciences and explores social-emotional topics in ways that connect with kids. Jessica is regularly featured in and contributes to media outlets on topics related to kids, parenting, and friendship. For more information, visit www.JessicaSpeer.com

"We are all a little weird and life's a little weird, and when we find someone whose weirdness is compatible with ours, we join up with them and fall in mutual weirdness and call it love."

—Dr. Seuss

About Familius

Visit Our Website: www.familius.com

Familius is a global trade publishing company that publishes books and other content to help families be happy. We believe that the family is the fundamental unit of society and that happy families are the foundation of a happy life. We recognize that every family looks different, and we passionately believe in helping all families find greater joy. To that end, we publish books for children and adults that invite families to live the Familius Ten Habits of Happy Family Life: *love together, play together, learn together, work together, talk together, heal together, read together, eat together, give together,* and *laugh together.* Founded in 2012, Familius is located in Sanger, California.

Connect

Facebook: www.facebook.com/familiustalk
Twitter: @familiustalk, @paterfamilius1
Pinterest: www.pinterest.com/familius
Instagram: @familiustalk

FAMILIUS

The most important work you ever do will be within the walls of your own home.